SLAVE and CITIZEN

SLAVE
and
CITIZEN

FRANK TANNENBAUM
With an Introduction
by Franklin W. Knight

BEACON PRESS
BOSTON

To J.B.T.

Beacon Press
25 Beacon Street
Boston, Massachusetts 02108–2892

Beacon Press books
are published under the auspices of
the Unitarian Universalist Association of Congregations.

Published by arrangement with Alfred A. Knopf, Inc.

First digital print edition 2001

Library of Congress Cataloging-in-Publication Data

Tannenbaum, Frank, 1893–1969.
Slave and citizen / Frank Tannenbaum ; with an
introduction by Franklin W. Knight
p.   cm.
Reprint. Originally published: New York : Alfred A. Knopf, 1946.
ISBN 0–8070–0913–X (paper)
1. Blacks—America—History.   2. Slavery—America—
History.   3. America—Race relations.   I. Title.
E29.N3T3   1991
973'.0496—dc20   91–21434

INTRODUCTION

FRANK Tannenbaum (1893–1969) was a most remarkable scholar; and *Slave and Citizen* remains a
most remarkable book. First published in 1947, it
reflected the vibrant characteristics that made Frank
Tannenbaum such an outstanding teacher, scholar,
and advocate. He was bold, combative, articulate,
passionate, highly curious, widely read, and enormously energetic. He also possessed an extremely in-
cisive mind.

Born in Poland, Frank Tannenbaum arrived in the
United States at an early age. His youthful intellectual formation came from living in New York City
and attending Columbia University where he earned
his bachelor's degree in 1921. Even if Columbia University had not been such an exceptionally distinguished intellectual place during those war- and early
postwar years, New York City would still certainly
have made an indelible impression on Tannenbaum,
who remained throughout his life an impressionable
and enormously sensitive individual. Few cities were
more dynamic than New York in the first three de-
cades of the twentieth century. Jervis Anderson's
This Was Harlem captures the incessant action of
the city at that time. Teeming with recent arrivals
from the South and a great number of foreign countries, New York was rapidly changing in size, com-

position, culture, and character and in its insatiable capacity for flamboyance. With their city regarded as the commercial, cultural, and intellectual mecca of the United States, New Yorkers exhilarated in diversity and change. New York was also an overtly political city, sympathetic to a wide array of political opinions, especially those considered liberal or left of center. Living in the city was itself a sort of education, but Tannenbaum had certified credentials as well.

Before he earned his doctoral degree in 1927 from the Robert Brookings Graduate School in Economic and Political Science (and with some experience in political organizing in New York City), Tannenbaum set out for Mexico which at that time was still slowly recovering from the widespread chaos of its disastrous revolution. At a time when most Americans were avoiding Mexico as too dangerous, Tannenbaum found it an exciting place to be. He worked enthusiastically for the Mexican government, traveled tirelessly throughout the country, and became inextricably fascinated not only by the variety of people and places of Mexico but also by all of Latin America. No scholar in his lifetime did more than Frank Tannenbaum to introduce Latin American societies and Latin American history to a U.S. audience. Tannenbaum's insatiable reading, traveling, and writing about Latin America inevitably gave him a more cosmopolitan appreciation for the history of the entire hemisphere. Moreover, he remained convinced that comparative history could illuminate some of the basic domestic problems of the United States. This context eventually produced *Slave and Citizen.*

Two years after he joined the faculty of Columbia University in 1936, Frank Tannenbaum inaugurated what later became—as he explains in his acknowledgments—the University Seminars with an interdisciplinary discussion on "the history of slavery in the Western World." It was a timely topic. The 1930s were profoundly disturbing years for the United States as they were for most of the rest of the world. The Great Depression, coming on the heels of the Great Crash, had virtually devastated the national economy and demoralized a great number of the people. The country was extremely agitated. Then came the consoling, ameliorative legislation of the New Deal, a program in which Frank Tannenbaum played a role. The New Deal was designed not only to aid in recovery and relief measures but also to prevent any recurrence in American society of such unfortunate social and economic consequences. The political and economic institutions established under the Franklin D. Roosevelt administration permanently altered the nature as well as the role of government in the everyday lives of citizens. This was especially true in the second phase of the New Deal, in the controversial years after 1935, when the government attempted to implement various social and economic legislative measures aimed at benefiting the working classes.

One group that did not benefit tangibly from the various remedial measures of federal, state, and local government was the growing number of citizens of African ancestry. Indeed, after the short-lived creative involvement of what Nathan Huggins and others before and after would call "The Harlem Renaissance" of the 1920s, African Americans found themselves more rudely, harshly, and savagely discriminated against and excluded than at any time since the Civil War.[1]

The racial situation was serious enough that in 1937 the Carnegie Corporation of New York commissioned the Swedish sociologist Gunnar Myrdal to undertake "a comprehensive study of the Negro in the United States."[2] Myrdal's project, partly interrupted by the Second World War, became an extensive interdisciplinary and interracial one. It involved the leading scholars at that time, the young and the old, the well known and the promising—Ruth Benedict, Franz Boas, Vincent Brown, Ralph Bunche, Kenneth Clark, St. Clair Drake, W. E. B. DuBois, E. Franklin Frazier, Melville Herskovits, Charles Johnson, Otto Klineberg, Ruth Landes, Alain Locke, Hortense Powdermaker, Ira DeA. Reid, Edward Shils, Richard

---

[1] See Nathan Irvin Huggins, *Harlem Renaissance* (New York: Oxford University Press, 1971).

[2] Gunnar Myrdal. *An American Dilemma: The Negro Problem and Modern Democracy* (New York: Harper and Row, 1944), p. li.

Sterner, Walter White, and Donald R. Young. Most would continue to make a tremendous impact on American scholarship in the postwar years. Moreover, some of the outstanding studies on African Americans published by Harper Brothers in the 1940s resulted from the team assembled by Myrdal. These included Melville Herskovits, *The Myth of the Negro Past* (1941), Charles Johnson, *Patterns of Negro Segregation* (1943), Richard Sterner, *The Negro's Share* (1943), and Otto Klineberg, *Characteristics of the American Negro* (1944).[3] The Carnegie Corporation study attempted, with only limited success, to integrate in one coherent presentation, the best available scholarship on African Americans in the United States. This reversed the tradition of generally neglecting the works of able, distinguished black scholars such as W. E. B. DuBois, Carter G. Woodson, and Charles H. Wesley.[4]

It is an understandable coincidence, then, that Frank Tannenbaum, ever curious and current, should have assembled a small number of scholars in 1938–39 to examine carefully what was then regarded as an "American problem." Tannenbaum never fully explained the relationship of that seminar to his book, but when he set about writing he certainly gave the

---

[3] According to Myrdal's report, the manuscripts and other memoranda of the team were deposited in the Schomburg Library.

[4] See M. Thomas Inge, Maurice Duke, and Jackson R. Bryer, eds., *Black American Writers: Bibliographical Essays* (New York: St. Martin's Press, 1978).

subject a different twist. Tannenbaum focused on what he termed the moral relation. "Slavery," he wrote, "was not merely a legal relation; it was also a moral one. It implied an ethical bias and a system of human values, and illustrated more succinctly, perhaps, than any other human experience the significance of an ethical philosophy." He was supremely confident that the moral angle was the single most useful window to explore the general social attitudes toward the institution of slavery. "For if one thing stands out clearly from the study of slavery, it is that the definition of man as a moral being proved the most important influence both in the treatment of the slave and in the final abolition of slavery."

In examining the problem of slavery Frank Tannenbaum again demonstrated those exemplary characteristics of the trained historian and of the sensitive as well as sensible individual that had marked his previous writings, especially his extensive work on Mexico. He liked the long time span, the careful concern for geographical variation, and the comparative examination of peculiar circumstances. History was past but relevant for the present and the future.

Slave and Citizen is a short work. It was not, however, hastily written; it was carefully and thoroughly thought through. The bibliographical research for its time was impressive. It was not what we would today define as basic research utilizing primary sources, exemplified by the Johns Hopkins University Studies done under the direction of Herbert Baxter Adams at the end of the nineteenth and the beginning of the twentieth century.[5] It was a succinct synthesis of enormous wisdom. As was Tannenbaum's method he read just about everything published on the subject in English, Spanish, French, Portuguese, and German. He consulted the standard works such as Bryan Edward's *The History, Civil and Commercial, of the British Colonies in the West Indies* (1806); James Bandinel's *Some Account of the Trade in Slaves From Africa* (1842); Alexander Humboldt's *The Island of Cuba* (1856); and Sir Harry Johnston's *The Negro in the New World* (1910). He pored through printed editions of the *Siete Partidas*, the compilations of the brilliant King Alfonso X of Castile and Leon, and several editions of Spanish laws and government documents. His meticulous footnotes include V. Martin de Moussy's *Description . . . de la Confédération Argentine* (1860); Dieudonné P. Rinchon's *La Traité et l'esclavage des Congolais par les Européens* (1929); the undated J. P. Oliviera Martins's *O Brasil e as Colonias Portuguesas;* and Werner Sombart's *Der Moderne Kapitalismus* (1922).

Two recently published books (and a long and interesting conversation with Professor William West-

---

[5] On the Johns Hopkins Studies, see Stanley M. Elkins, *Slavery: a Problem in American Institutional and Intellectual Life*, 2d ed. (Chicago: University of Chicago Press, 1968), pp. 8–9. First edition published in 1959.

ermann) especially influenced Tannenbaum. The first was *Capitalism and Slavery* (1944) by Eric Williams, an Oxford University Graduate and then member of the faculty at Howard University. The second was *O Mundo que O Portugues Criou* (1940) by Gilberto Freyre, whom Tannenbaum obviously admired.[6] In Williams's work Tannenbaum appreciated the importance of economic influences on social relations. "The slave trade was a great economic enterprise," he wrote, "but the long term consequences were beyond the ken of the men involved in it." Freyre's work reinforced Tannenbaum's impression that the Iberian world produced a different colonial variant from that of the northwest Europeans.

Frank Tannenbaum was not complacent with the publication of *Slave and Citizen*. It was not his manner to accept anything as definitive, least of all his own work. "As I look at this little book upon a great subject," he wrote resignedly in his introduction, "I find that I am more unhappy now that it is finished than I was when writing it. It raises more questions, by implication at least, than it answers. And the questions it raises are those that trouble our own day. They are questions of freedom, liberty, justice, law, and morality. All of them revolve around the place of man in the world and the relation of men to each other." Frank Tannenbaum shared an inherent mod-

---

[6] Freyre's book still remains untranslated into English.

esty with all truly great thinkers: he accepted grace-
fully the corrections that later scholars made to the
basic assumptions and even some facts included in
Slave and Citizen. Many scholars have challenged the
estimate of "twenty million human beings" sold into
slavery.[7] Many have also challenged the notion that
Iberian-American colonies provided a more sympathetic and conducive atmosphere for manumission and
acceptance of ex-slaves into the society. Viewed sys-
tadially (that is, at comparable stages of socioeconomic
development) rather than synchronically (that is, at
the same period of time), the African experience in
Spanish and Portuguese America may have differed
in degree but not fundamentally in kind from that
found elsewhere. The conditions of life on sugar plantations, wherever and whenever those plantations existed throughout the Americas, were generally "nasty,
brutish, and short." Regardless of how Iberian Catholics may have endowed their slaves with a "moral personality" it could not mitigate the essential horror and
brutality of the system.

---

[7] The text is a bit ambiguous here. Tannenbaum speaks of
"victims" rather than slaves, a term that could possibly include
the widespread domestic disruption in African communities. The
most reliable estimates of Africans landed in the Americas are
closer to ten million. See Philip D. Curtin, *The Atlantic Slave
Trade: A Census* (Madison: University of Wisconsin Press, 1969)
and Paul E. Lovejoy, "The Volume of the Atlantic Slave Trade:
A Synthesis," in *The Journal of African History* 23 (1982):
473–501, which includes the various calculations and modifications
since 1969.

Nevertheless, *Slave and Citizen* remains among the most influential books ever published about slavery, a prominent historiographical landmark. Despite some minor shortcomings—more the result of its early timing rather than deficiencies of the author—it remains essential reading and a standard in any good bibliography. It formed the basis for Stanley Elkins's *Slavery: A Problem in American Institutional and Intellectual Life* (1959), as well as Herbert Klein's *Slavery in the Americas: A Contemporary Study of Virginia and Cuba* (1967). Winthrop Jordan refers to *Slave and Citizen* as a "seminal study" in his *White over Black: American Attitudes toward the Negro, 1550–1812* (1968). The book also features in such outstanding studies as David Brion Davis's Pulitzer Prize–winning *The Problem of Slavery in Western Culture* (1966) and Eugene D. Genovese's *The World the Slaveholders Made* (1969).

A good book is one that continually excites its field, stimulates discussion, and provokes debates. *Slave and Citizen* has certainly done that. It invites not mindless agreement but intellectual respect. That is the secret of its success; and that is why Frank Tannenbaum's words will continue to resonate from generation to generation.

FRANKLIN W. KNIGHT
The Johns Hopkins University

AUTHOR'S INTRODUCTION

As I look at this little book upon a great subject I find that I am more unhappy now that it is finished than I was when writing it. It raises more questions, by implication at least, than it answers. And the questions it raises are those that trouble our own day. They are questions of freedom, liberty, justice, law, and morality. All of them revolve about the place of man in the world and the relation of men to each other. Slavery was not merely a legal relation; it was also a moral one. It implied an ethical bias and a system of human values, and illustrated more succinctly, perhaps, than any other human experience the significance of an ethical philosophy. For if one thing stands out clearly from the study of slavery, it is that the definition of man as a moral being proved the most important influence both in the treatment of the slave and in the final abolition of slavery. Once it was believed that all men are free by nature and equal in the sight of God, once the doctrine of the spiritual identity of all men, slave or free, came to rule men's minds and condition their legal sys-

tem, then the very nature of slavery came to reflect the accepted doctrine.

The idea of the moral value of the individual outlasted slavery and became the chief source of its undoing. This belief has persisted throughout the last two thousand years. It is the chief heritage of the Western, the European world, and the very survival of European culture — perhaps of the European man — depends upon the survival of this doctrine. If it were to be lost, the European scheme of values would be lost with it.

There is in the history of slavery an important contribution to the theory of social change. Wherever the law accepted the doctrine of the moral personality of the slave and made possible the gradual achievement of freedom implicit in such a doctrine, the slave system was abolished peacefully. Where the slave was denied recognition as a moral person and was therefore considered incapable of freedom, the abolition of slavery was accomplished by force — that is, by revolution. The acceptance of the idea of the spiritual equality of all men made for a friendly, an elastic milieu within which social change could occur in peace. On the other hand, where the slave was denied a moral status, the law and *the* mores *hardened and became stratified, and their historical outcome proved to be violence and revolution. But the bearing upon social policy and social change of the idea of the moral equality of all men would require a much longer book than the one here offered to the reader.*

FRANK TANNENBAUM

Columbia University

ACKNOWLEDGMENTS

LIKE every book, this one is a child of its own time, and the author's indebtedness is much wider than he can specify. Indirectly but immediately the study stems from a seminar on the history of slavery in the Western World, first given at Columbia University in 1938–9 by Professors William L. Westermann, Geroid T. Robinson, John A. Krout, and the author. This seminar has proved important because it brought to bear upon a common theme the historical experience of different cultures, and especially because it was the first attempt at what has since become at Columbia, the University Seminars, of which there are now five, in the fields of Religion, the State, Peace, the Renaissance, and Rural Life and Education. These seminars attempt to integrate all of the disciplines and experience that relate to a given institution or to a given field of knowledge.

I also wish to acknowledge my indebtedness to Lyman Bryson and to Professors Charles W. Cole and Robert Livingston Schuyler.

I am under obligation to Mrs. Dorothea Boardman for getting the book ready for press.

SLAVE and CITIZEN

SLAVE AND CITIZEN

THE settling of the Western Hemisphere by peoples coming from Europe and Africa was an adventure on a grand scale, involving diverse peoples, varying cultures, millions of human beings, and hundreds of years. The common element was the New World, though strangely dissimilar in physical features and cultural type. But the student discerns many an analogous design, patterned by the newcomers as they established themselves in the strange and unexplored regions. It is natural, therefore, for Gilberto Freyre to mark revealing identities between the history of Brazil and that of the United States.[1] Like everything that Gilberto Freyre writes, *Brazil: An Interpretation* has a freshness and lucidity that endow the reader with insight and understanding of the complex instrumentalities for life and labor contrived by man in his new world. Freyre finds, among other similarities in the development of Brazil, the impact of the frontier and the dominion of the plantation so typical of our own South. The disparity

---

[1] Gilberto Freyre: *Brazil: An Interpretation* (New York: Alfred A. Knopf; 1945).

3

4

implied rather than expressed in the study is the divergent position of the Negro within the two areas. For in Brazil the Negro, and especially the mulatto, had an access to the culture and a role in social life unknown in the United States. In politics, in the arts, and in society the mulatto found the door ajar, even if not fully open, and a markedly different social milieu has come into being. Even under the Empire the Negro and the mulatto — and, socially, the attractive mulatto women — had an acceptance unthinkable in the American scene. Freyre quotes from Ewbank this revealing picture:

I have passed black ladies in silks and jewelry, with male slaves in livery behind them. Today one rode past in her carriage, accompanied by a liveried footman and a coachman. Several have white husbands. The first doctor of the city is a colored man; so is the President of the Province.[2]

In another place [3] he points out that gentlemen of dark color achieved the dignity of president of the cabinet under the Emperor.

A social atmosphere so dissimilar in two nations built in the New World by immigrants from the Old challenges analysis. It cannot be a mere accident. The way these two societies have gone must have an explainable etiology, and an examination of the source of the difference may illumine the present.

---

[2] Thomas Ewbank: *Life in Brazil, or the Land of the Cocoa and the Palm* (London, 1856), p. 266.

[3] Gilberto Freyre, op. cit., p. 101.

We are really concerned with one of the major race and population problems of the Western Hemisphere. The Negro is found everywhere in this hemisphere except Greenland, and there are regions where he is so numerous that long ago Humboldt spoke of a possible colored empire in the Caribbean. From Rio de Janeiro northwards, the coastal stretches of Brazil, French, Dutch, and British Guiana, Venezuela, Colombia on both the Atlantic and the Pacific, Ecuador, and Peru have significant and in certain districts preponderant numbers of people of African origin. This same holds true for both coasts in Central America. In Mexico the Negro on the coastal plains has largely merged with the Indian population, but even here traces of African influence are still visible, while our Southern states, bordering on the Gulf of Mexico, the Mississippi, and the Atlantic, have a colored population of many millions, which in some rural sections outnumbers the whites. Even Canada and Alaska have a fraction of Negroes in their population. It is on the islands in the Caribbean, however, rather than on the mainland of North or South America, that the Negro has acquired a dominating place. If Humboldt's reference is taken in a demographic rather than a political sense, the colonization of the Western Hemisphere has involved the settlement of many thousands of square miles by peoples come from Africa rather than from Europe, and if we draw an arc from Rio de Janeiro to Washington, D.C., and include the West Indian islands within it, we shall have, in outline, the empire Humboldt talked about.

The enumeration of the colored people in the Western Hemisphere can be only approximate. The definition of Negro and mulatto varies in different countries; the census records are incomplete in some, and out of date in others. But in spite of that, even a rough estimate will help fix the magnitude of the problem. There are more than 13,000,000 Negroes in the United States, or 12 per cent of the total population. Humboldt, at the beginning of the nineteenth century, adjudged the colored population of all the Antilles at 2,360,000, or 83 per cent of the total.[4] The more immediate record reveals the British, French, and Dutch possessions and the Virgin Islands as almost completely colored. Of the largest islands, Barbados, with 174,774, has 7 per cent white; Jamaica, with perhaps a million, only 2 per cent of full European stock; and Trinidad, with 387,425, perhaps 4 per cent Caucasian. Of all the other British West Indies, only one, St. Kitts, with 18,730 people, has as many as 6 per cent white. The rest have less than 5 per cent. (Nevis, the Virgin Islands, and Grenada have only 1 per cent of their population, or less, white.)[5] One thing is clear: that the British West

---

[4] Alexander Humboldt: *The Island of Cuba*, translated from the Spanish by J. S. Thrasher (New York, 1856), p. 186.

[5] W. M. Macmillan: *Warning from the West Indies* (London: Faber & Faber; 1936), p. 186.

Indies belong demographically to people of African rather than European origin. These same conditions prevail in the French and Dutch Caribbean islands. Martinique, out of a population of over 240,000, has between three and four thousand whites.[6] Very similar conditions prevail in Guadeloupe[7] and in the minor islands. The Dutch islands, including Curaçao, have between 80 per cent and 90 per cent Negro and mulatto.[8]

Only Cuba, Puerto Rico, and Santo Domingo are not completely dominated by the colored race. For reasons too complex to explain here, these areas were retained, in part at least, as a European habitat. In Santo Domingo the white population is said to be 13 per cent of the total, the Negro 19 per cent, and the rest mixed,[9] whereas Cuba, in spite of the fact that in the first quarter of the nineteenth century it had more Negroes and mulattoes than whites, counts at present about 27 per cent colored out of a population of about four million.[10] While Puerto Rico has 25.7 per cent colored,[11] the population of Haiti is al-

---

[6] Raye R. Platt, John K. Wright, John C. Weaver, and Johnson E. Fairchild: *The European Possessions in the Caribbean Area* (New York: American Geographical Society; 1941), p. 53.

[7] Ibid., p. 60.　　　　　[8] Ibid., p. 74.

[9] *Refugee Settlement in the Dominican Republic* (Washington, D.C.: Brookings Institution; 1942), p. 86.

[10] *Problems of the New Cuba* (New York: Foreign Policy Association; 1935), p. 27.

[11] U. S. Census of 1930, *Outlying Territories and Possessions*, Table 2, p. 136.

most completely colored. The proportion of European population in the Guianas is only fractional, and the Negro and mulatto population of Brazil is very large. The identification of the mulatto as white, and the tendency to speak of the Negro as being whitened out in Brazil, make most contemporary statements misleading. But we do have some historical evidence that tells its own tale. In 1817 there were, out of a population of 3,617,900, only 843,000 whites and 2,887,500 Negro freedmen and slaves, not to count another 628,000 mestizos — which in this case means mixtures of whites, Negroes, and Indians. The rest were pure Indians.[12] This was before the very large importation of Negroes between that date and 1850, which has been estimated at between three and five million. In 1884 the number of slaves is given as 3,000,000.[13] Even Simonsen, who tends to understate the importance of the Negro slave in Brazil, says that in the eighteenth and nineteenth centuries there were 1,000,000 employed in sugar, 600,000 in mining, 250,000 in coffee, and 1,100,000 in other employments.[14]

The Argentine, which boasts of being pure European, would merely forget the record. For more than

---

[12] Balbi: *"Essai statistique sur le Royaume de Portugal,"* quoted in Roberto C. Simonsen: *Historia Economica do Brasil 1500–1820* (São Paulo, 1937), Vol. II, p. 56.

[13] Sir Harry Johnston: *The Negro in the New World* (London: Methuen & Co.; 1910), p. 98.

[14] Roberto C. Simonsen, op. cit., p. 205.

two and a half centuries the Negro was an important element in the total population. The number of Negroes in Argentina cannot be accurately known because of the absence of records and because of the extensive smuggling. Buenos Aires had become a port of illegal entry of Negro slaves on their way to Peru and, we must presume, to Argentina as well. One item alone tells a significant tale. In the port of Buenos Aires, for only the twenty years 1606–25, 8,925 Negroes of illegal entry were denounced, and, when sold, produced 1,384,709 pesos, of which the crown received 745,443 pesos as its share, the rest going to the informers and to the judges.[15] This little item illuminates an entire social complex and makes understandable assertions so often repeated that all work is done by the Negroes as the whites will do none of it.

In 1634 the *cabildo* of Buenos Aires instructed its agent in Madrid to ask for permission for travelers to Peru, Tucumán, or Chile to take Negro servants with them as there were no Indians in Buenos Aires that could be used for that purpose.[16] Father Carlos Gervasoni, of the Order of Jesus, writing in 1729, estimates the number of people in the city of Buenos Aires at 24,000, and says that at least one third of that

[15] Manuel Ricardo Trelles: "Hernandarias de Saavedra," *La Revista de Buenos Aires*, T. IX (Buenos Aires, 1866), p. 424.

[16] "*Instruccion que el Cabildo de Buenos Aires remite á su apoderado en Madrid*," *La Revista*, op. cit., T. VI, p. 136.

number are African Negro slaves. "Our college alone
will have over three hundred." All things pass
through their hands, because there is not a Spaniard
here, no matter "how miserable," who will not put on
"a wig and a sword." [17] At about the same time Father
Cayetano Cattaneo says that "These [the Negroes]
are the only ones in all of these provinces who serve
in the houses, work in the fields, and at all of the other
trades. If it were not for the slaves, it would not be
possible to live here, for no Spaniard, no matter how
poor, will . . . serve. . . . They do all . . . and
are . . . excellent craftsmen [in building], so that
Buenos Aires is taking on such a form that the Europeans will not be able to look down upon her with dis-
dain." [18]

Father Chome,[19] of the Order of Jesus, tells us that

---

[17] Father Carlos Gervasoni: *"Carta al Padre Comini de la
Compañia de Jesus," La Revista,* op. cit., T. VIII, pp. 177–8.

[18] *"Carta del Padre Cayetano Cattaneo, abril, 1730,"* ibid.,
pp. 315–6, 319.

[19] *Cartas Edificantes, y Curiosas, Escritas de las Misiones Es-
trangeras, y de Levante por Algunos Missioneros de la Compañia
de Jesus,* traducidas por el Padre Diego Davin, de la Misma Compañia. T. XIII (Madrid, 1756), p. 300. *"Carta del Padre Chome,
Sept. 1730, Missionero de la Compañia de Jesus, al Padre Van-
thiennen, de la Misma Compañia":*

*"Habia en Buenos Ayres mas de veinte mil Negros, y Negras,
á quienes faltaba toda instrucción, porque no sabían la Lengua
Española. Como los mas eran de Angola, Congo, y Loango, me dió
gana de aprender la Lengua de Angola, la qual está en uso en
dichos tres Reynos. Salí con mi empeño, y en menos de tres meses*

he spent a year in Buenos Aires learning the African tongues and evangelizing the Negroes, who did not know Spanish, and he estimates them at 20,000 — a number that, if correct, would place the colored population at well over half of the total, as the city at that time had less than 40,000 inhabitants.

In 1773 [20] in Tucamán all the houses had large numbers of Negro slaves, and in Córdoba a thousand slaves were sold from only two haciendas owned by religious houses. Among these Negroes were many musicians, and others skilled in all of the various crafts. The Convent of Saint Theresa had a ranch with 300 male and female slaves, while many private houses had as many as thirty or forty slaves.

The first census of the Republic of Argentina [21] cites the formal record of 1778, indicating that one third of the population consisted of people of color, while de Moussy gives 6,000 for Buenos Aires in 1770, out of a total population of 22,000, and 7,000 for Córdoba in 1778. The total estimated by de Moussy [22] is 30,-000 for all of Argentina in that period. But, what-

---

me puse en estado de oír sus confessiones, tratar con ellos, y explicarles todos los Domingos la Doctrina Christiana en nuestra Iglesia."

[20] "El Lazarillo de Ciegos Caminantes," originally published in 1773. *Biblioteca de Cultura Peruana,* Ser. I, No. 6 (Paris, 1938), p. 66.

[21] *Primer Censo, de la República Argentina* (Buenos Aires, 1872), p. 10.

[22] V. Martin de Moussy: *Description . . . de la Confédération Argentine,* Vol. II (Paris, 1860), p. 239.

ever the exact number, it is clear that the Negroes
were numerous and important. They not only did all
of the physical labor about the houses and towns, were
the craftsmen in building and other crafts, but became
important in the rural districts as "*gauchos*." A colored
or mulatto gaucho appears in the literature and in the
traveler's accounts, and we find Gillespie [23] writing
of a certain *hacendado* who owned 60,000 head of
cattle, and eighty Negroes who did nothing but de-
vote their time to the care of his cattle. Don Francisco
de Aguirre [24] tells us that in 1783 "almost all the
people of service are slaves," and in 1852 Sir Woodbine Parish [25] writes: "The porters, carters, carriers,
drivers, and all of the washerwomen of Buenos
Aires are free Negroes and Mulattoes." In 1815, in
Corrientes, "Some of the ladies brought *mulatillas*,
little female slaves with them; and, these either remained at the door, looking in upon the company, or

---

[23] Major Alexander Gillespie: *Gleanings and Remarks, Col-
lected during Many Months of Residence at Buenos Ayres and
within the Upper Country* (Leeds, 1818), p. 144.

[24] "*Diario de Don Francisco de Aguirre,*" *Anales de la Biblioteca,* T. IV, L. 3, Cap. 2 (Buenos Aires, 1900), p. 173.

[25] Sir Woodbine Parish: *Buenos Ayres* and the Provinces of
the Rio de la Plata: from their discovery and conquest by the
Spaniards to the establishment of their political independence.
With some account of their present state, trade, debt, etc.; an ap-
pendix of historical and statistical documents; and a description
of the geology and fossil monsters of the pampas (London: J.
Murray; 1852, 2nd Edition), p. 56.

if very young, squatted at their mistress's feet in the room." [26]

Toward the end of the colonial period, Venezuela, in a population of approximately 1,000,000, had 72,-000 Negro slaves and 400,000 mulattoes, or something over 47 per cent of African origin.[27] There were few in Paraguay, perhaps less than 2 per cent of the total population.[28] Chile at the beginning of the nine-teenth century had 30,000 Negroes and mulattoes out of a population of about half a million,[29] whereas in Peru there were well over 100,000 just at the end of the eighteenth century,[30] while in what is now Ecuador there were 50,000, and in Colombia, 210,-000.[31]

While statistical tables of racial composition in the population are always misleading, at least in the sense that they give an impression of finality that they do not possess, they are, when carefully done, somewhat

[26] J. P. and W. P. Robertson: *Letters on South America, Comprising Travels on the Banks of the Paraná and Rio de la Plata*, Vol. I (London, 1843), p. 56.

[27] Arcaya: *Estudios de Sociologia Venezuelana*, p. 470.

[28] Natalicio Gonzalez: *Proceso y Formación de la Cultura Paraguaya* (Buenos Aires, 1930), p. 36.

[29] Domingo Amunategui Solor: "*La Trata de Negros en Chile*," *Revista Chilena de Historia y Geográfica*, Vol. XLIV (October 1922), p. 39.

[30] Ricardo Donoso: *El Marqués de Osorno don Ambrosio Higgins, 1720–1801* (Santiago de Chile, 1941), p. 465.

[31] José Manuel Restrepo: *Historia de la Revolución de la República de Colombia* (10 vols., Paris, 1827), Vol. I, p. 216.

useful as a source of reference. The following table will help summarize and make graphic the magnitude of the problem we are here considering.

The sum of these figures amounts to 41,140,719 people of color in the Western Hemisphere. Even if only relatively accurate, they are sufficiently impressive to call for a reconsideration of the role of the African people in this hemisphere. The settlement of America was not a purely European enterprise. It is more accurately described as a common undertaking by the folk coming from both Europe and Africa. For the slave trade is better viewed as a migratory movement — forced migration, if you will, but still one of the greatest population movements of all time. This movement stretched over more than four centuries (1442–1880) and was integrally related to the colonization of large parts of the Western Hemisphere.

Negro migration to Europe from Africa began in 1442, half a century before the discovery of America.[32] In 1443 there was a shipment of 235 slaves to Portugal.[33] In 1448 the first "factory" was established in the island of Arguim for the purpose of the new commerce. By 1461 the trade had been regular-

---

[32] Fray Bartolome de Las Casas: *Historia de las Indias*, Tomo I, Cap. 24, p. 129 (Madrid, n. d.). Bryan Edwards: *History of St. Domingo* (Edinburgh: J. Pillans & Sons; 1802), p. iii. J. P. Oliveira Martins: *O Brazil e as Colonias Portuguezas* (Lisbon, n. d.).

[33] J. Lúcio de Azevedo: *Épocas de Portugal Económico* (Lisbon: Livraria Classica Editora; 1929), p. 71.

ized and was carried on peacefully in Senegambia, and the island of Arguim alone supplied, during the later half of the fifteenth century, an average of seven to eight hundred slaves per year.[34] What had hitherto been an internal migration in Africa had now become water-borne, first to Europe across the Mediterranean and later, with the discovery of America, across the Atlantic to the New World. African participation in the new world adventure began early, and in 1501 Nicholas Ovando, the new Governor of Española, is advised to import Negroes born in Christian lands.[35] The first fifty Negroes from Africa were brought to the Antilles in 1511, and by 1517 the trade had been so well established that a regular *"asiento"* was given to the Governor of Bressa to introduce 4,000 Negroes to America. The migration to America did not interrupt the flow to Portugal itself, and in 1552, in a population of 100,000, Lisbon had some 10,000 slaves, with from sixty to seventy slave markets. There were among them, 1,550 washerwomen, 1,000 street cleaners, and 400 who peddled crabs, cooked rice, and other delicacies.[36]

From this time on, the movement was in full swing,

---

[34] J. P. Oliveira Martins, op. cit., p. 71.

[35] *Colección de Documentos Inéditos, Relativos ai descubrimiento, conquista y organización de las Antiguas Posesiones Españolas de América y Oceania, sacados de los Archivos del Reino, y muy especialmente de Indias,* T. XXXI (Madrid: Frias & Co.; 1888), p. 23.

[36] J. Lúcio de Azevedo, op. cit., pp. 75–6.

THE AMERICAN POPULATION IN 1940

	Indians	%	Mestizos	%	Negroes	%	Mulattoes	%	Total
NORTH OF MEXICO									
Greenland	17,557	97.54	Included in Indians				Included in Negroes		18,000
Alaska	32,464	44.86			150	.21			72,361
Canada	128,000	1.12			20,559	1.80			11,422,000
United States	361,816	0.27			13,455,988	12.01			131,669,275
TOTAL	539,387	0.37			13,476,697	9.42			143,181,636
MEXICO, ANTILLES, CENTRAL AMERICA									
Mexico	5,427,396	27.91	10,619,496	54.61	80,000	0.41	40,000	2.04	19,446,065
Antilles	200	0.07	10,000	....	5,500,000	39.29	3,000,000	21.43	14,000,000
Guatemala	1,820,872	55.44	985,280	30.00	4,011	0.12	2,000	0.06	3,284,269
British Honduras	2,938	5.00	5,875	10.00	15,000	25.55	20,000	34.03	58,759
Honduras	105,732	9.54	775,501	70.00	55,275	4.99	10,000	0.90	1,107,859
El Salvador	348,907	20.00	1,308,401	75.00	100	.0001	100	.0001	1,744,535
Nicaragua	330,000	23.90	828,172	60.00	90,000	6.52	40,000	2.88	1,380,287
Costa Rica	4,200	0.64	65,612	10.00	26,900	4.09	20,000	0.14	656,129
Panama	64,960	10.28	135,604	21.47	82,871	13.12	271,208	42.91	631,549
TOTAL	8,105,205	19.03	14,733,941	34.82	5,854,157	13.84	3,403,308	8.04	42,309,452
SOUTH AMERICA									
Colombia	147,300	1.60	4,234,890	46.00	405,076	4.50	2,205,382	24.32	9,206,283
Venezuela	100,000	2.79	2,000,000	55.86	100,000	2.79	1,000,000	27.93	3,580,000
English Guiana	15,000	4.39	10,000	2.93	100,000	29.30	80,000	23.44	341,237

Country									Total
Dutch Guiana	00,000	33.71	10,000	5.01	17,000	9.55	20,000	11.23	177,950
French Guiana	10,000	25.00	2,000	0.50	1,000	0.25	1,000	0.25	40,000
Ecuador	1,000,000	40.00	900,000	36.00	50,000	2.00	150,000	6.00	2,500,000
Peru	3,247,196	46.23	2,247,395	32.00	29,054	0.41	80,000	0.71	7,023,110
Bolivia	1,650,000	50.00	990,000	30.00	7,800	0.26	5,000	0.15	3,300,001
Brazil	1,117,132	2.70	4,135,660	10.00	5,789,924	14.00	8,276,321	20.01	41,356,605
Paraguay	40,000	4.16	672,000	70.00	5,000	0.52	5,000	0.52	960,000
Uruguay	Extinct		100,000	4.66	10,000	0.46	50,000	2.30	2,145,545
Chile	130,000	2.58	3,014,123	60.00	1,000	0.02	3,000	0.06	5,023,539
Argentina	50,000	0.38	1,312,972	10.00	5,000	.038	10,000	.076	13,129,723
TOTAL	7,566,628	8.52	19,629,040	22.10	6,520,854	7.34	11,885,703	13.38	88,784,023
SUMMARY									
North of Mexico	539,837	0.37	Included in Indians		13,476,697	9.41	Included in Negroes		143,181,638
Mexico, Antilles, Central America	8,105,205	19.03	14,733,941	34.82	5,854,157	13.84	3,403,308	8.04	42,309,452
South America	7,566,628	8.52	19,629,040	22.10	6,520,854	7.34	11,885,703	13.40	88,784,023
TOTAL IN AMERICA IN 1940	16,211,670	5.91	34,362,981	12.52	25,851,708	9.42	15,289,011	5.56	274,275,111

Adapted from Angel Rosenblatt: *La Población indígena de América, desde 1492 hasta la actualidad* (Buenos Aires: Institución Cultural Española; 1945).
NOTE: This is the most recent and the best-documented history of racial distribution in the Western Hemisphere.

and all of the European nations facing the Atlantic were drawn into it to a greater or lesser extent, and for longer or shorter periods. The Portuguese, the French, the Dutch, the English, the Danes, the Swedes, the Spaniards, and even Brandenburg participated in it, while on the Atlantic side the American colonies, Brazil, and Cuba at one time or another imported Negroes on their own account.

The first in the slave traffic were the Portuguese. They had begun as early as the first quarter of the fifteenth century tentatively to search out the African coast, by opening the Canary and the Madeira Islands to Portuguese settlement, and by 1434 rounded Cape Bojador, reaching Rio d'Ouro (Río d'Oro) in 1436, and from then on pushed along the coast to Sierra Leone, the Grain, Ivory, and Gold Coasts, to the mouth of the Niger and the islands of St. Thomas and Fernando Po, finally crossing the Equator. The African coast for four thousand miles, from the Senegal River in the north to the southern port of Angola beyond the Equator, now lay open to the white slave-trader. He came to tap this inexhaustible source of black labor and carry it in ever increasing numbers across the ocean to work in his strange and unexpected New World. A commerce grew up on a vast scale in which human beings from Africa were bartered for goods manufactured in Europe. These goods were of varied and curious assortment, specialized and particularized for different parts of the African coast. On the Leeward coast the trade goods were iron bars, crystal beads, corals, and brass-mounted cutlasses. Brass basins were required on the Ivory Coast. Copper and iron bars were needed on the Slave Coast and at Calabar. Arms, gunpowder, tallow, sheets, cotton and serge fabrics from Europe and the East Indies, spirits, and beads were of general use. Special care had to be devoted to the color scheme of the goods because the Negroes were very particular and had specialized tastes. Illustrations of this nice discrimination is seen in the fact that anything blue was rejected on the Gambia, while only blue aggry beads were acceptable on the Gold Coast. They also preferred the "perpetuanas" to be yellowish green.[37]

The slave trade, as can be seen, was an extensive and, by all accounts, a profitable commerce in which for centuries European and American merchants bartered goods for Negro slaves. The goods employed were varied, and were largely drawn from England; the ships, the merchants, the sailors, and the finances came from all of the leading commercial nations that had ships at sea. A few examples drawn mainly from English sources will indicate the lucrative character of the trade.

In the eleven years between 1783 and 1793 Liverpool put 878 ships into trade, shipped 303,737 Ne-

---

[37] Hon. H. A. Wyndham: *The Atlantic and Slavery*, "Problems of Imperial Trusteeship" series (London: Oxford University Press; 1935), p. 66.

groes from Africa, at a value of £15,186,850.[38] Deductions for various commissions, and other charges, gave Liverpool a gross return of $12,294,116, or £1,700,000 per year. After all necessary expenses in transporting and insurance were calculated, it was estimated that there was a gain of 30 per cent on every slave sold. Liverpool, therefore, received a net income in the eleven slave years of over £2,300,000 on the 303,737 Negroes, or an annual rate of over £200,000. In effect the annual return pervaded the whole town and contributed to the support of the greater part of the inhabitants. Almost everyone in Liverpool had some share in the trade. It is well known that many of the smaller vessels that imported about a hundred slaves were fitted out by attorneys, drapers, grocers, tallow-chandlers, bankers, tailors, and so on. Some had one eighth, some a sixteenth, and some a thirty-second share in the undertaking.[39]

While there were between twenty-five and forty-two recognized houses in the trade in any one year, ten of these during the eleven-year period sent out 502 ships of 878 that departed from Liverpool be-

---

[38] "Dicky Sam": *Liverpool and Slavery*, by a genuine "Dicky Sam" (Liverpool: A. Bosker & Son; 1884), cites thirteen years between 1771 and 1806 when more than a hundred ships sailed in the slave trade every year out of Liverpool alone.

[39] "A General Descriptive History of Liverpool," quoted in Elizabeth Donnan: *Documents Illustrative of the History of the Slave Trade to America* (Washington, D.C., Carnegie Institution of Washington; 1930).

tween 1783 and 1793, inclusive. How important the trade was to Liverpool may be deduced from the fact that one half of all the shipping in that port was engaged in African trade in 1744.[40] Even the most conservative estimate of the net income on five ships shows that the *Lottery* in 1802 produced a net profit of £11,039, or over £23 per slave; the *Enterprise* showed over £6,428, or an average per slave of over £16; the *Fortune*, in 1805, over £1,877, or more than £5 per slave; and the *Louisa*, in the same year, a net profit of more than £8,500.[41]

The slave trade not only was profitable in itself, but gave rise to numerous industries in Great Britain and other countries to supply the goods needed in barter. It employed thousands of ship carpenters, joiners, ironmongers, painters, sailmakers, braziers, boatbuilders, coopers, riggers, plumbers, glaziers, gunsmiths, bread-makers, carters, and laborers, and used a good deal of copper for ships' bottoms.[42] The trade, in addition, not merely made possible the development of the British West Indies sugar colonies, but supplied the agricultural labor for vast areas in tropical South America and in the cotton and tobacco region of the United States. It was considered as "the great pillar and support of the British plantation trade," and Sir Josiah Child computes that every

---

[40] "Dicky Sam," op. cit., p. 104.
[41] Elizabeth Donnan, op. cit., p. 631, note.
[42] "Dicky Sam," op. cit., p. 83.

Englishman who went to the West Indian colonies employed eight or ten Negroes, and that their feeding, clothing, and equipping supported four men in England, while an Englishman emigrating to New England would not help support even one man at home.[43] And a recent study has detailed the importance of the slave trade in developing British cities like Liverpool and laying the foundations for the initial capital that went into the early Industrial Revolution in England.[44] The slave trade was a great economic enterprise, but its long-run consequences were beyond the ken of the men involved in it.

The trade was extensive and profitable, but exceeding cruel. The business developed its own special ways, adapted to the human cargo in which it dealt, and a kind of opaqueness to human suffering and sorrow grew upon those engaged in it that would be hard to believe if the record were not full beyond conjecture. That such things should have been possible at all is indicative of a capacity for callousness on the part of the human being that our own time has made fully evident. It is difficult to write of the slave trade with restraint, for until the day before yesterday we of the European tradition had a certain commitment to morality and a certain capacity for indignation at unwonted brutality. We of our day have become less

---

[43] William Law Mathieson: *British Slavery and Its Abolition* (London: Longmans, Green & Co.; 1926), p. 2.

[44] Eric Williams: *Capitalism and Slavery* (Chapel Hill, 1944).

sensitive to unkindness, more accustomed to seeing the human body racked and tortured without being benumbered by sheer horror. But with us, at least so we hope, this is a temporary abberation that will soon have passed away. The slave trade, on the other hand, lasted for over four centuries and involved, in some measure, all of the nations of Europe and many in this hemisphere, and counted among its victims perhaps as many as twenty million human beings.

Little Negro villages in the interior of Africa were frequently attacked in the middle of the night, the people were either killed or captured by Europeans themselves or, more frequently, by Africans acting on their own account or for Europeans, and the victims left alive were shackled with a collar about the neck, men, women, and children, and driven for hundreds of miles to the coast. This human caravan, guarded by armed men, with the leaders of the expedition carried in hammocks or litters, would sometimes trek a thousand miles through forest and jungle before reaching the stations where the Negroes destined for the slave trade could be disposed of. There they were assembled in stockades and kept against the time when a European slaver would arrive loaded with "African goods," for the purpose of bartering these human beings for the iron bars, the beads, and the cloth brought for the purpose. Such a ship might have loaded up in Liverpool, Nantes, Amsterdam, Bridgeport, or any other city engaged in the commerce. The

Negroes were mainly young, ranging somewhere between sixteen and thirty years of age. When the ship
was loaded to capacity it started on the journey across
the seas to the New World. A ship usually required
some nine months for a round trip; but if the weather
was bad, or if the ship's captain found upon reaching
the African station that he had been preceded by another ship in the trade, and the factory had no available cargo, then more time might be required. Under
those conditions the ship would load up with what it
could buy, and, throwing the black creatures into the
hold, would either wait for a new batch of Negroes to
arrive or cast off and seek to fill the ship at another
supply station. It is a matter of record that some ships
spent six months trying to fill their holds with Negroes, moving from port to port on the hot African
coast, with their living cargoes pining away between
decks or in the hold. When the ship had finally been
filled, it set out to vend its living wares in some ready
market on the other side of the Atlantic. But if misfortune followed in the track of the ship, the prospective market might be overcrowded with new Negroes
just delivered by another ship in the trade, and the
captain, with an eye to the profit of the trip, would
trek from island to island in the West Indies until he
finally disposed of his human cargo.

On the ship itself the men and women were crowded
between decks, with little air and less ventilation except such as filtered through narrow ventilators. There

they were kept at least fifteen or sixteen hours a day
— on good days, that is — in darkness, without modern systems of sanitation, and without running water,
naked, and with chains about their ankles. Two men
were chained together, as a rule the right ankle of one
to the left ankle of another. And, thus crowded and
bound hand and foot, they were allowed a space
barely larger than a grave — five feet six inches long,
sixteen inches broad, and two to three feet high, not
high enough to sit up in.[45]

---

[45] "During the discussion of the possible regulation of slave
vessels, Captain Perry visited Liverpool and examined eighteen
vessels, nine of which belonged to James Jones. . . . The dimensions of the 'Brookes,' one of the vessels examined, were:
'Length of lower deck, gratings and bulkheads included, 100
feet, breadth of beam on lower deck inside, 25 feet 4 inches,
depth of hold, from ceiling to ceiling, 10 feet, height between
decks, from deck to deck, 5 feet 8 inches, length of the men's
room, on the lower deck, 46 feet, breadth of the platforms in the
men's room on each side, 6 feet, length of the boys' room, 13 feet
9 inches, breadth of the boys' room, 25 feet, breadth of platforms
in boys' room, 6 feet, length of women's room, 28 feet 6 inches,
breadth of women's room, 23 feet 6 inches, length of platforms
in women's room, 28 feet 6 inches, breadth of platforms in
women's room, 6 feet, length of the gun-room, on the lower deck,
10 feet 6 inches, breadth of the gun-room on the lower deck, 12
feet, length of the quarter-deck, 33 feet 6 inches, breadth of the
quarter-deck, 19 feet 6 inches, length of the cabin, 14 feet, height
of the cabin, 6 feet 2 inches, length of the half-deck, 16 feet 6
inches, height of the half-deck, 6 feet 2 inches, length of the platforms, on the half-deck, 16 feet, 6 inches, breadth of the platforms on the half-deck, 6 feet, upper deck.
"Let it now be supposed that the above are the real dimensions

The men and women were kept apart on the voyage, and if the weather was clear and calm, the Negroes were allowed out on deck about eight in the morning and stayed there until five in the afternoon. But if it was stormy and rough and cold, then they lived in the stench beneath deck — dark, steaming, slimy, and wet.

. . . The height, sometimes, between decks, was only eighteen inches; so that the unfortunate human beings could not turn round, or even on their sides, the elevation being less than the breadth of their shoulders; and here they are usually chained to the decks by the neck and legs. In such a place the sense of misery and suffocation is so great, that the Negroes, like the English in the black-hole at Calcutta, are driven to frenzy. They had on one occasion, taken a slave vessel in the river Bonny: the slaves were stowed in the narrow space be-

---

of the ship 'Brookes,' and further, that every man slave is to be allowed six feet by one foot four inches for room, every woman five feet ten by one foot, every boy five feet by one foot two, and every girl four feet six by one foot, it will follow that a slave vessel will be precisely the representation of the ship 'Brookes,' and of the exact number of persons neither more nor less, that could be stowed in the different rooms of it upon these data. These, if counted, will be found to amount to four hundred and fifty-one. Now, if it be considered that the ship 'Brookes' is of three hundred and twenty tons, and that she is allowed to carry by act of Parliament four hundred and fifty-four persons, it is evident that if three more could be wedged among the number represented in the plan, this plan would contain precisely the number which the act directs."

Quoted by Elizabeth Donnan, op. cit., Vol. II ("The Eighteenth Century," 1931), p. 592 footnote.

tween decks, and chained together. They heard a horrid din and tumult among them, and could not imagine from what cause it proceeded. They opened the hatches and turned them up on deck. They were manacled together, in twos and threes. Their horror may be well conceived, when they found a number of them in different stages of suffocation; many of them were foaming at the mouth, and in the last agonies, — many were dead. The tumult they had heard, was the frenzy of those suffocating wretches in the last stage of fury and desperation, struggling to extricate themselves. When they were all dragged up, nineteen were irrecoverably dead. Many destroyed one another, in the hopes of procuring room to breathe; men strangled those next them, and women drove nails into each other's brains. Many unfortunate creatures, on other occasions, took the first opportunity of leaping overboard, and getting rid, in this way, of an intolerable life.[46]

When the weather cleared away and the hatches were opened, the stench was such as to overcome those unused to it.

The stench below was so great that it was impossible to stand more than a few minutes near the hatchways. Our men who went below from curiosity, were forced up sick in a few minutes; then all the hatches were off. What must have been the sufferings of those poor wretches, when the hatches were closed! I am informed that very often in these cases, the stronger will strangle the weaker; and this was probably the reason why so many died, or rather were found dead the morning after the capture. None but an eye witness can form

[46] Rev. R. Walsh: *Notices of Brazil* (Boston: Richardson, Lord & Holbrook; 1831), Vol. II, p. 265.

a conception of the horrors these poor creatures must endure in their transit across the ocean.[47]

But when the day was clear, they were taken out, given water to wash their hands and face, and a little lime juice to cleanse their mouth, and food — Indian corn, yams, barley, and biscuit. On cold days a little rum was passed about, and when the weather permitted, they were doused in salt water to keep them well and given a little palm oil to rub their bodies with. And the story runs that, all going well, they were given native musical instruments and encouraged to play their native songs, to sing and to dance, with their shackles on — or perhaps these were taken off for the occasion.

In case of rebellion and mutiny, the punishment was swift, summary, and sure: hanging to the mast or walking the plank. And then, when the day's sun began to set, the innocent and surely very bewildered Negroes, who had been forced from the interior of Africa into a white man's purgatory, on their way to an unknown and unforeseeable destination, were driven back into the dark between the decks, to wait the dawning of another day with its unknown future. If the weather was favorable and the ship in good hands, and the trip was comparatively short, the men arrived on the American coast with few losses. But if

[47] Quoted by Lawrence F. Hill: *Diplomatic Relations between the United States and Brazil* (Durham, N. C.: Duke University Press; 1932), p. 133.

the ship had bad luck, rough weather, or a poor master and was also the carrier of some contagious disease, then the devil himself could have worked no greater havoc among men. There are cases on record of the larger part of the men dying of disease, of ships running out of water and being forced to cast men overboard to save the rest, of mutiny in which riot and murder ran rampant:

> Some eight or ten of them were shot, with small shot, in the hold of the brig before they could be subdued. Some thirty or forty of them were then brought on deck and two and two in irons, were hung up at the yard-arm, shot, their bodies let down, and then their arms and legs chopped off to get the irons off the corpses, and one woman was thrown into the sea before life was extinct.[48]

Finally, when the slave trade was abolished and the carrying of Negroes from Africa to America became illegal, then the ships were built for speed, the crowding became even worse if possible, and the barbarities more unmitigated, for at the fear of being captured by war sloops doing guard duty on the African coast or along the approaches to the West Indies or Brazil, captains were known to have cast their Negroes into the sea to escape detection; and there are records of as many as five hundred Negroes on one of these ships being cast overboard for the sharks in the wake of the ship to devour.

When the ship drew close to the shores of the

---

[48] Quoted in Lawrence F. Hill, op. cit., p. 134.

Western World there was a systematic effort to heal the abrasions on the Negroes' bodies and to polish their skin with substantial applications of oil. The arrival in port was announced in advance by the firing of a gun, and the crowd of purchasers rushed upon the ship and manhandled the frightened Negroes lined up for inspection. So great was the confusion and fright sometimes produced that Negroes had been known to jump overboard in sheer fright at the new and unpredictable meaning of the sudden excitement. The Negroes desired were marked out by the would-be purchaser by some sign, and the frightened, naked creatures were looked over, measured, felt, and haggled about like cattle at any market, and finally sold to some purchaser, who would then decorate his prize with a hat and a handkerchief and march him off to be branded. That was the process in its bare details by which the Negro was carried from Africa to America. Once here, he still had to go through the "seasoning," which always exacted a heavy mortality.[49]

It is difficult to calculate the loss in lives exacted by the slave trade. All figures are estimates, but it has been said that about one third of the Negroes taken from their homes died on the way to the coast and at the embarkation stations, and that another third died crossing the ocean and in the seasoning, so that only

---

[49] Bryan Edwards: *The History, Civil and Commercial, of the British Colonies in the West Indies* (Philadelphia: James Humphreys; 1806), Vol. II, p. 330.

one third finally survived to become the laborers and colonizers of the New World.

The number of Negroes transported will never be known. The subjection of the trade to fiscal ends by various governments led to extensive contraband, and the more officers there were set to watch the law-breakers, the more participants in the illegal traffic there came to be. Nor did the abolition of the slave trade by Great Britain and the United States, in 1807, end the traffic. If anything, it may have increased it. For it is clear from the records that both Cuba and Brazil imported greater numbers annually after that date than before it. In fact, the transfer of Negroes did not cease until the abolition of slavery itself, not only in the United States, but in Cuba in 1880 and in Brazil in 1888, and even then it continued out of Africa to Sãn Thomé.[50] Portugal, which had been the first to enter the trade, was the last to leave it. There is no way of giving even seeming accuracy to the numbers of slaves imported, but a rough estimate may be had from citing the record for individual countries and periods.

Between 1511 and 1513, 1,265 Negroes of both sexes passed through the "Casa do Escravos" in Lisbon for the account of the King, and the Jesuit Father Garcia Simoëns,[51] describing the active com-

---

[50] Sir Harry Johnston, op. cit., p. 84.

[51] Dieudonné P. Rinchon: *La Traité et l'esclavage des Congolais par les Européens* (Bruxelles, 1929), p. 59.

merce out of Angola in 1576, estimates the annual export from there alone at 12,000. Between that year and 1591, 52,000 were shipped to Brazil; [52] the British West Indies, between 1680 and 1786, imported 2,130,000; [53] the French West Indies had an annual import, between 1780 and 1789, of 30,000; and Cuba, between the years 1790 and 1820, 225,574,[54] and from 1821 to 1847, an average annual number of some 6,000 to 7,000,[55] not counting those smuggled in. The total numbers up to 1853, for Cuba alone, has been stated to be over 644,000,[56] and we know that the importations continued after that.[57]

Records for individual years are scattered, but suggest large annual exports out of Africa. In 1769 more than 97,000 Negroes were embarked for America,[58] while testimony before the House of Commons on the effect of the abolition of the slave trade commented that it would reduce the demand for slaves by seventy or a hundred thousand, as the slave trade

---

[52] Dieudonné P. Rinchon, op. cit., p. 63.

[53] Bryan Edwards, quoted by Amos K. Fiske: *The West Indies* (New York: G. P. Putnam's Sons; 1899), p. 105.

[54] Alexander Humboldt, op. cit., p. 218.

[55] J. P. Oliveira Martins, op. cit., p. 62.

[56] Alexander Humboldt, op. cit., p. 219, footnote by translator.

[57] William R. Manning (ed.): *Diplomatic Correspondence of the United States.* Vol. XI, *Spain, 1854* (Washington, 1939), p. 765. *United States Foreign Relations, 1865,* Part I, p. 665.

[58] Werner Sombart: *Der moderne Kapitalismus,* Erster Band (Leipzig, 1922), p. 703.

carried on with the East through Egypt involved only between 1,500 and 2,000 Negroes.[59]

For Brazil, the importations all through this period were large and increasing. Between 1759 and 1803 the exports to Brazil from Angola are said to have amounted to 642,000, or an annual average of 14,000 or 15,000.[60] Some Brazilian writers have put the numbers imported at an annual rate of 44,000 for the seventeenth century and 55,000 for the eighteenth.[61] The imports into Brazil continued heavy until about 1850, and have been placed as high as 50,000 per year for the ten years between 1842 and 1852.[62]

All general figures are guesses, but the estimates are significant. One author[63] estimates the general migration from the Congo to America to have been as follows: 7,000 annually during the sixteenth century, 15,000 during the seventeenth, and 30,000 during the eighteenth; for the first half of the nineteenth century he places the number at the incredible sum of 150,000 annually to 1850, and as high as 50,000 be-

---

[59] Henry Brougham: *An Inquiry into the Colonial Policy of the European Powers*, Vol. I (Edinburgh, 1803), p. 566.

[60] J. P. Oliveira Martins, op. cit., p. 62.

[61] Pandía Calogeras: *Formacão Historica do Brasil* (Rio de Janeiro, 1930), p. 53.

[62] Percy Alvin Martin: "Slavery and Abolition in Brazil," in the *Hispanic American Historical Review*, Vol. XIII, No. 2 (May 1933), p. 159.

[63] Dieudonné P. Rinchon, op. cit., p. 133.

tween 1850 and 1860, and 2,000 between 1860 and
1885, a total of more than 13,000,000 from the Congo
from the beginning of the commerce. Exaggeration,
it seems — but, how much? Another author [64] sug-
gests a total of 20,000,000 exported from all Africa
for the entire period. Again an exaggeration? But by
how much? Even a conservative estimate would
hardly cut this figure in half. It really makes little
difference how much it is cut, for, to repeat, the enterprise lasted over four centuries and engaged the
energies of many commercially minded people in
many parts of Africa, Europe, and the Western Hemisphere.

Some check on these generalizations is provided by
scattered records of the number of ships engaged in
the traffic. Toward the last third of the eighteenth
century, there were forty factories on the African
coast belonging to the leading nations in Europe engaged in the African trade. Of those, ten belonged
to the English, three to the French, fifteen to the
Dutch, four to the Portuguese, and four to the
Danes.[65] Each of these nations had ships of its own
plying the Atlantic, carrying Negroes across the
ocean. In 1600 and later,[66] more than a hundred
Spanish and Portuguese ships entered Loanda every

---

[64] J. P. Oliveira Martins, op. cit., p. 64.
[65] Bryan Edwards, op. cit., Vol. II, p. 255.
[66] Dieudonné P. Rinchon, op. cit., p. 68.

year, while [67] 192 British ships were used in the year 1771 to bring 47,146 Negroes to the West Indies.[68] In 1788 the French engaged 98 ships to carry over 29,000 slaves to Santo Domingo.[69] Long after the active campaign to abolish the slave trade had been under way, there were recorded, for the period between 1833 and 1840, anywhere from 33 to 50 ships a year entering the ports of Cuba loaded with Negroes from Africa.[70] American-built vessels to the number of sixty-four were sold in Rio de Janeiro alone in 1845, and most of them were put to the slave trade; [71] as late as 1848,[72] vessels sailed in the slave trade from Bahia.

The slave trade was a profitable business and it attracted speculators and adventurers from many lands. A slave could be sold in Cuba for thirty times what he had cost in Africa,[73] and as long as a market could be had, there were people ready to satisfy it even if the trade had been outlawed and the risks were great. Joint stock companies were formed to promote expeditions to Africa, and the flag of one nation or

---

[67] Bryan Edwards, op. cit., p. 258.

[68] "Dicky Sam," op. cit.

[69] Henry Brougham, op. cit., pp. 530–1.

[70] James Bandinel: *Some Account of the Trade in Slaves from Africa* (London, 1842), p. 232.

[71] Lawrence F. Hill, op. cit., p. 129.

[72] William Hadfield: *Brazil, the River Plate, and the Falkland Islands* (London, 1854), p. 147, note.

[73] William Law Mathieson, op. cit., p. 161.

another was used, through fictitious sales, to evade the law. The traders operating changed their flag to fit changing circumstances and, after the English outlawed the trade, operated first under the French flag, then under the Spanish and the Portuguese, and then the American.

Our refusal to concede the right of search had the effect of playing into the hands of those who were engaged in the traffic. The three years from 1859 to 1862 saw at least 170 expeditions fitted for the trade; 74 of these were believed to have sailed from New York, 43 from other American ports, 40 from Cuba, and the rest from Europe.[74] The situation had become so much of a scandal that President Buchanan said in his message to Congress of May 19, 1860: "It is truly lamentable that Great Britain and the United States should be obliged to expend such a vast amount of money and treasure for the suppression of the African slave trade, and this when the only portions of the civilized world where it is tolerated and encouraged are the Spanish islands of Cuba and Porto Rico." [75]

It can be seen from even these fragmentary illustrations — and they could be very greatly increased — that the ships were numerous and the trade was continuous. How many ships, on an average, sailed annually during the four centuries? The ships were

---

[74] William Law Mathieson, op. cit., p. 165.

[75] James D. Richardson: *A Compilation of the Messages and Papers of the Presidents, 1789–1897*, Vol. V, p. 595.

not large and most of them, perhaps, carried fewer than 300 Negroes at a time. Toward the later part of the eighteenth century, it is true, there were ships that carried 500 or more Negroes on a single voyage, but on the whole these were exceptions. If we put the average at 300 Negroes per voyage — and that would probably be an exaggeration — it must have taken many hundreds of ships in the trade to carry the total number of men across the Atlantic. Hundreds of ships, thousands of sailors, and hundreds, perhaps thousands, of individuals, partnerships, and companies were engaged in bringing to the New World south of the United States more Africans than Europeans for the entire colonial period.

The Negro, much against his will, was to become a participant in the building of the New World. The migration continued for so long a time because of the heavy mortality: "almost half of the new imported Negroes die in the seasoning, nor does the polygamy which they use add much to the stocking of a plantation"; [76] because in parts of the New World the Negro did not reproduce, and because men were more readily welcomed than women for the heavy labor. On the average, only one woman was imported for every three men. There were plantations in Cuba, for instance, that had as many as seventeen males to one female, and the females became common wives, pros-

---

[76] Charles Leslie: *A New and Exact Account of Jamaica* (Edinburgh, 1739), p. 328.

titutes, incapable of bearing children or unwilling to do so. The life of the Negro plantation laborer in the West Indies is said to have averaged seven years, and replenishment went on at the rate of one seventh or one eighth per year.[77] If the migration had been by families, it would perhaps have been smaller in numbers and of shorter duration.

Everything conspired to keep the slave trade alive for long centuries. It would seem simple and natural to assume that the slaves brought to this hemisphere would multiply in such numbers as to make it unnecessary to keep on dragging bewildered Negroes from their distant homes in the depths of Africa across the ocean to maintain the requisite labor supply in the West Indian sugar islands. But local African custom, the profits of the trader, the needs of the planter, and the barrenness of Negro women under slave conditions, all combined to impose the need for continued importation of Negroes to supply a labor market always being depleted. Polygamy in Africa made fewer "salable" women available for the market; the young females taken in slave raids were kept for wives and the males were sold. Older women — that is, women over twenty-two or three — were not readily acceptable, whereas a well-proportioned man of even thirty-five might find a ready purchaser. The plantation-owners needed field hands for the sugar plantations, and the work was too exacting for women. While the

[77] Werner Sombart, op. cit., p. 702.

tendency was for all plantations to have some women on them, their number was almost never equal to that of males. Even on the Cuban sugar estates, where one would expect marriage to have been encouraged for religious reasons, there came to be a practice of keeping male slaves only, and this was justified on the grounds that it kept down vicious habits.[78]

The readier market for males made it necessary for the law to require shipmaster to include one third females among the Negroes they brought from Africa. The failure of the Negro in the sugar colonies to reproduce himself is illustrated by the record from Jamaica. In 1690 that island had about 40,000 slaves, and between that date and 1820 it imported about 800,000 more. And yet in 1820 the island had only 340,000.[79] Many attempts were made, especially toward the end of the slave trade, to increase the number of women on the plantations, notably in Cuba, but without much effect.[80] It is not clear that even if the women had been more nearly equal in number to the men, the natural increase under the special conditions of slavery in the British West Indies would have been the result. One thoughtful and observant Jamaica plantation-owner, who was eager for his slaves to in-

---

[78] Alexander Humboldt, op. cit., p. 213.

[79] Frank Wesley Pitman: "Slavery on British West Indian Plantations in the Eighteenth Century," in the *Journal of Negro History*, Vol. XI (1926), p. 631.

[80] Alexander Humboldt, op. cit., p. 214.

crease by natural growth, as the English slave trade had already been abolished and the plantations in the islands were being abandoned for lack of labor, did what he could to favor the Negro women who had children, and yet he complains over and over again that all his solicitude seemed of no avail. The Negro women did not have children.

This morning (without either fault or accident) a young, strong healthy woman miscarried of an eight months' child; and this is the third time that she has met with a similar misfortune. No other symptom of childbearing has been given in the course of this year, nor are there above eight women upon the breeding list out of more than one hundred and fifty females. Yet they are all well clothed and well fed, contented in mind, even by their own account, over-worked at no time, and when upon the breeding list are exempted from labor of every kind. In spite of all this, and their being treated with all possible care and indulgence, rewarded for bearing children, and therefore anxious themselves to have them, how they manage it so ill I know not, but somehow or other certainly the children do not come.[81]

It is a matter of record that in twelve years before the abolition of the slave trade a report for eleven British West Indian islands showed a decline in the slave population of over 60,000.[82] And yet as soon as slavery was abolished, the population tide turned and the number of Negroes on the islands began to in-

[81] M. G. Lewis: *Journal of a West India Proprietor, 1815–17* (London, 1929), pp. 314–5.

[82] "The West Indies, as They Were and Are," in the *Edinburgh Review* (April 1859), p. 220.

crease. On ten of these same islands the number of Negroes increased by 54,000 in the next twelve years.[83]

Despite the cost in life, sorrow, and broken bodies, the Negro became the effective means for the colonization of vast American regions. Cotton and tobacco in the United States, sugar in the West Indies, cocoa in Venezuela, sugar, mining, and coffee in Brazil, and a thousand other kinds of enterprise everywhere else were dependent upon the Negro. In Brazil the Negro was so much the laborer that no one else seemed to labor at all, and until very recently it was considered unseemly even to carry a small parcel in the city of Rio. As Mawe puts it, in Brazil the Negro seemed to be the most intelligent person he met because every occupation, skilled and unskilled, was in the Negroes' hands. Even in Buenos Aires theirs was the hand that built the best churches. They were the fieldhands, and in many places the miners; they were the cooks, the laundresses, the mammies, the concubines of the whites, the nurses about the houses, the coachmen, and the laborers on the wharves. But they were also the skilled artisans who built the houses, carved the saints in the churches, constructed the carriages, forged the beautiful ironwork one sees in Brazil, and played in the orchestras. The Negro, slave and free, was the living hand that embellished the setting and provided the art and the spice for the cultured, easy, and care-

---

[83] Ibid., loc. cit.

free life that some of the New World plantation centers luxuriated in for so long a time. The very pattern so characteristic of a large section of colonial and post-colonial life in this hemisphere derived from their skills, their loyalty, and their participation in the world about them, even as slaves.

Without the Negro the texture of American life would have been different — different in lore, family, social organization, and politics and, equally important, different in economy. Conceivably even the crops that the Negro cultivated in gangs, and sometimes under the lash, would not have been grown at all, and large parts of tropical and semitropical American land would have remained untilled and unnurtured. Viewed from any side — biologically, in terms of physical labor, socially, and in the molding of the culture so typical of the Western World — the Negro, for those areas where he labored and lived in large numbers, was just as important as his master, and his contribution to the population and settlement of this hemisphere is part of a common adventure of folk from across the sea who have molded a new and a different social milieu for themselves. American colonization is, therefore, a joint Afro-European enterprise.

Looked at from the Negro's point of view, it has been a good adventure. For in spite of the slave trade, in spite of the horrors of the middle passage, in spite of the centuries of slavery, the Negro has accommodated himself to the New World in a manner not merely creditable, but surprising. The Indian, on the other hand, has either withered away and disappeared, as he did in the West Indies, or been killed and driven off, as in the plains of the United States and Argentina. Where he has not been extirpated from the earth, he has remained mostly a pariah in his native habitat. Compare the Negro in Cuba and Brazil with the Indian in Peru, for example. The Negro in Cuba and in Brazil is an active member of the body politic; in Peru the Indians form an isolated body, apart from the rest. Whereas the Negro has learned the language of the European, the Indians, by the millions, have remained stubborn, uncommunicative, and isolated in their own linguistic universe. The same has happened with many other elements of European culture — dress, food, social customs, song, art, and matters of faith. The Negro is a magistrate on the city bench of New York, a member of Congress; he is a senator and a member of the cabinet in other places. He is part of the nation. He is active, vocal, self-assertive, and a living force. He has become culturally a European, or, if you will, an American, a white man with a black face. The Indian, where he has survived in large numbers, as in Guatemala, for instance, has not become identified in this way — it might be said in any way — with the European. For those things he has taken over he has so amalgamated with his own native customs that their European origin is hard to recognize.

But this adventure of the Negro in the New World has been structured differently in the United States than in the other parts of this hemisphere. In spite of his adaptability, his willingness, and his competence, in spite of his complete identification with the *mores* of the United States, he is excluded and denied. A barrier has been drawn against the Negro. This barrier has never been completely effective, but it has served to deny to him the very things that are of greatest value among us — equality of opportunity for growth and development as a man among men. The shadow of slavery is still cast ahead of us, and we behave toward the Negro as if the imputation of slavery had something of a slave by nature in it. The Emancipation may have legally freed the Negro, but it failed morally to free the white man, and by that failure it denied to the Negro the moral status requisite for effective legal freedom.

But this did not occur in the other parts of this world we call new and free. It did not occur because the very nature of the institution of slavery was developed in a different moral and legal setting, and in turn shaped the political and ethical biases that have manifestly separated the United States from the other parts of the New World in this respect. The separation is a moral one. We have denied ourselves the acceptance

of the Negro as a man because we have denied him
the moral competence to become one, and in that have
challenged the religious, political, and scientific bases
upon which our civilization and our scheme of values
rest. This separation has a historical basis, and in turn
it has molded the varied historical outcome.

The Negro slave arriving in the Iberian Peninsula
in the middle of the fifteenth century found a propitious environment.[84] The setting, legal as well as
moral, that made this easy transition possible was due
to the fact that the people of the Iberian Peninsula
were not strangers to slavery. The institution of
slavery, which had long since died out in the rest of
western Europe, had here survived for a number

---

[84] Elizabeth Donnan, op. cit., Vol. I ("1441–1700," 1930),
p. 29: "For as our people did not find them hardened in the belief
of the other Moors, and saw how they came in unto the law of
Christ with a good will, they made no difference between them
and their free servants, born in our own country. But those whom
they saw fitted for managing property, they set free and married
to women who were natives of the land, making with them a division of their property, as if they had been bestowed on those
who married them by the will of their own fathers, and for the
merits of their service they were bound to act in a like manner.
Yea, and some widows of good family who bought some of these
female slaves, either adopted them or left them a portion of their
estate by will, so that in the future they married right well, treat-
ing them as entirely free. Suffice it that I never saw one of these
slaves put in irons like other captives, and scarcely any one who
did not turn Christian and was not very gently treated." Quoted
from *The Chronicle of the Discovery and Conquest of Guinea*,
by Gomes Eannes de Azurara.

of reasons, especially because of the continuing wars
with the Moors, which lasted until the very year of
the discovery of America. At the end of the fifteenth
century there were numerous slaves in Portugal and
Spain, and especially in Andalusia, among them not
only Negroes, but Moors, Jews, and apparently Spaniards as well.[85] For we have records of white slaves
sent to America by special permission of the crown.
We know that Rodrigo Contreras, the Governor of
Nicaragua, was allowed by special *cedula,* of July 15,
1534, to import two white slaves; Fernando Pizarro
in 1535 was permitted four white slaves; and there
were a number of similar records.[86] There were large
numbers of Negro slaves in both Portugal and Spain.
By the middle of the sixteenth century Algarves was
almost entirely populated by Negroes, and they out-
numbered the whites in Lisbon.[87] In Spain, in 1474,
Ferdinand and Isabella empowered the Negro Juan
de Valladolid, known as the "Negro Count," as the
"mayoral of the Negroes," to settle their quarrels and
to enforce the King's justice among them.[88] But long
after this date there were still Moorish and Jewish
slaves in Spain. In 1500–1, Jewish slaves held by
Spaniards were required to be baptized or to be sent

[85] Dieudonné P. Rinchon, op. cit., p. 44.

[86] George Scelle: *La Traite négrière* (Paris: L. Lerose & L.
Tenin; 1906), Vol. I, pp. 219–20.

[87] H. Morse Stephens: *Portugal* (New York, 1891), p. 182.

[88] Arthur Helps: *The Spanish Conquest in America* (London,
1855), Vol. I, p. 32.

out of the country within two months. Slaves were
to be freed by baptism if their masters were Moors or
Jews.[89] As late as 1616 the law speaks of baptized
Moorish slaves.[90]

But the mere survival of slavery in itself is perhaps
less important than the persistence of a long tradition
of slave law that had come down through the Justinian
Code. The great codification of Spanish traditional
law, which in itself summarizes the Mediterranean
legal *mores* of many centuries, was elaborated by
Alfonso the Wise between the years 1263 and 1265.
In this code there is inherent belief in the equality of
men under the law of nature, and slavery therefore is
something against both nature and reason.[91] But the
doctrine of the equality of human nature had long
before been asserted by Cicero. According to him,
there is "no resemblance in nature so great as that between man and man, there is no equality so com-

---

[89] Henry Charles Lea: *A History of the Spanish Inquisition*
(New York, 1906), Vol. I, pp. 142–5.

[90] Ibid., Vol. III, p. 405.

[91] "*Servidumbre es postura et establescimiento qui ficieron
antiguamente las gentes, por la qual los homes, que eran natural-
miente libres, se facian siervos et se sometian a señorio de otri
contra razon de natura.*" Ley I, título xxi, partida 4, *Las Sieste
Partidas del Rey Don Alfonso el Sabio, Cortejadas con Variod
Codices Antiguos por la Real Academia de la Historia, y Glosadas
por el Lic. Gregorio Lopez, del Consejo Real de Insias de S. M.
Nueva Edición, precedida del Elogio del Rey Don Alfonso por
D. J. de Vargas y Ponce, y Enriquecida con su Testamento Po-
lítico* (5 vols., Paris, 1847).

plete." [92] Reason is common to all men, and all are equal in their capacity for learning. Under guidance, every race of men is capable of attaining virtue. This doctrine of the equality of man is applied to the idea of slavery by Seneca with great vigor. Virtue is immune to misfortune. "A slave can be just, brave, magnanimous." Slavery is the result of misfortune, and hateful to all men. But, after all, slavery affects only the body, which may belong to the master; the mind "cannot be given into slavery." [93] The soul of the slave remains free.

The slave is a man and suffers from the same pains, and delights in the same joys, that all men do. The slave, as a human being, is derived from the same source, and will finally come to the same end, as other men. The distinction between slavery and freedom is a product of accident and misfortune, and the free man might have been a slave. These theories of the equality of man were in the background when the New Testament and the Christian fathers came upon the scene and proclaimed that all men are equal in the sight of God. The conception of the identity of human nature over all the world is like that in Cicero and Seneca.[94] And when St. Paul touches upon the subject

---

[92] R. W. Carlyle and A. J. Carlyle: *A History of Mediæval Political Theory in the West* (Edinburgh and London: W. Blackwood and Sons; 1903), Vol. I, p. 8.

[93] Ibid., p. 21.

[94] Ibid., p. 84.

of slavery, it is to the effect that in the sight of God "there is neither bond nor free." [95] That is, in their brotherhood as children of one God, the bondsman and the master are equal in his sight. This does not involve a repudiation of slavery, but rather an assertion that spiritually they are equal. And when St. Paul sends Onesimus, apparently an escaped slave, back to his master, it is with the admonition that he should be received as "a brother beloved." [96] There is no suggestion of freedom for the returning slave, but rather that he should be received "as myself." [97] Slavery is not formally opposed: "Let every man abide in the same calling wherein he was called"; [98] but there is also a favoring of freedom: "Art thou called being a bond servant? Care not for it; but if thou mayest be made free, use it rather." [99]

St. Paul further develops the theme of the equality of master and slave: "Servants, be obedient to them that are your masters according to the flesh with fear and trembling, in singleness of your heart, as unto Christ. . . . And, ye masters, do the same things unto them, forbearing threatening, knowing that your Master also is in heaven; neither is there respect of persons with him." [100] There is perhaps no great dis-

---

[95] Galatians iii, 28.
[96] Philemon, 16.
[97] Ibid., 17.
[98] Corinthians viii, 20.
[99] Ibid. viii, 21.
[100] Ephesians vi, 5, 9.

tinction to be drawn between St. Paul's attitude toward the equality of man and that of Cicero and Seneca, but clearly the doctrine that slavery merely affects the outer man and that spiritually master and slave are equal is here reaffirmed, and was to "dominate the thought and practical tendencies of the church." [101] These underlying doctrines become part of the theory of the later church fathers, and take the form of saying that God made not slaves and free men, but all men free.

This belief that equality among men is natural and reasonable is, therefore, both pagan and Christian, and stems from the Stoics and from the Christian fathers. The conception that man is free and equal, especially equal in the sight of God, made slavery as such a mundane and somewhat immaterial matter. The master had, in fact, no greater moral status than the slave, and spiritually the slave might be a better man than his master. *Las Siete Partidas* was framed within this Christian doctrine, and the slave had a body of law, protective of him as a human being, which was already there when the Negro arrived and had been elaborated long before he came upon the scene. And when he did come, the Spaniard may not have known him as a Negro, but the Spanish law and *mores* knew him as a slave and made him the beneficiary of the ancient legal heritage. This law provided, among other matters, for the following:

---

[101] R. W. and A. J. Carlyle, op. cit., Vol. I, pp. 88–9.

The slave might marry a free person if the slave status was known to the other party. Slaves could marry against the will of their master if they continued serving him as before. Once married, they could not be sold apart, except under conditions permitting them to live as man and wife. If the slave married a free person with the knowledge of his master, and the master did not announce the fact of the existing slave status, then the slave by that mere fact became free.[102] If married slaves owned by separate masters could not live together because of distance, the church should persuade one or the other to sell his slave. If neither of the masters could be persuaded, the church was to buy one of them so that the married slaves could live together.[103] The children followed the status of their mother, and the child of a free mother remained free even if she later became a slave.[104] In spite of his full powers over his slave, the master might neither kill nor injure him unless authorized by the judge, nor abuse him against reason or nature, nor starve him to death. But if the master did any of these things, the slave could complain to the judge, and if the complaint were verified, the judge must sell him, giving the price to the owner, and the slave might never be returned to the original master.[105] Any Jewish or Moorish slave became free

---

[102] *Las Siete Partidas*, Ley I, tit. v, part. 4.
[103] Ibid., Ley II.   [105] Ibid., Ley III.
[104] Ibid., Ley II, tit. xxi, part. 4.

upon turning Christian, and even if the master himself later became a Christian, he recovered no rights over his former slave.[106]

Las Siete Partidas goes into considerable detail in defining the conditions under which manumission could occur. A master might manumit his slave in the church or outside of it, before a judge or other person, by testament or by letter; but he must do this by himself, in person.[107] If one of the owners of a slave wished to free him, then the other must accept a just price fixed by the local judge.[108] A slave became free against his master's will by denouncing a forced rape against a virgin, by denouncing a maker of false money, by discovering disloyalty against the King, by denouncing the murderer of his master.[109] The slave could become free if he became a cleric with the consent of his master, or in certain cases without his consent, providing another slave in his place. And if the former slave became a bishop, he had to put up two slaves, each valued at the price that he himself was worth, while still a slave.[110] A Christian slave living among the Moors might return to live among the Christians as a free man.[111]

The slave could appeal to the courts (1) if he had

---

[106] *Las Siete Partidas*, Ley VIII.
[107] Ibid., Ley VI, tit. xxii, part. 4.
[108] Ibid., Ley II.
[109] Ibid., Ley IV.
[110] Ibid., Ley IV.
[111] Ibid., Ley VII.

been freed by will and testament, and the document maliciously hidden; under these circumstances he could appeal against anyone holding him; (2) if the slave had money from another and entrusted it to someone for the purpose of being bought from his master and given his liberty, and if then this person refused to carry out the trust, by refusing either to buy him or to free him if he had bought him; and (3) if he had been bought with the understanding that he would be freed on the receipt of the purchase price from the slave, and refused either to accept the money or to release him after accepting it.[112] He could appeal to the courts for defense of the property or his master in his master's absence, and the King's slaves could appeal to the courts in defense of the King's property, or of their own persons — a special privilege permitted the King's slaves in honor of their master.[113] A man considering himself free, but demanded for a slave, might have a representative to defend him; a man held a slave, but claiming to be free, might argue his own case, but not have a representative, and he must be permitted to argue and reason his case; the slave's relatives might plead for him, and even a stranger could do so, for "all the laws of the world aid toward freedom." [114] Slaves could be witnesses, even against their masters, in accusations for treason against

---

[112] Ibid., Ley VII, tit. ii, part. 3.

[113] Ibid., Ley IX, tit. ii, part. 3.

[114] Ibid., Ley IV, tit. v, part. 3.

the King; in cases of murder of either master or mistress by either spouse; or in cases against the mistress for adultery; when one of the two owners of a slave was accused of killing the other; or in case of suspicion that the prospective heirs have killed the master of another slave.[115] A slave who became the heir of his master, in part or in totality, automatically became free.[116] If a father appointed a slave as the guardian of his children, the slave by that fact became free; [117] and if he was the slave of more than one person and became an heir of one of his masters, the other must accept a price in reason for that part of the slave which belonged to him.[118] He who killed his slave intentionally must suffer the penalty for homicide, and if the slave died as a result of punishment without intention to kill, then the master must suffer five years' exile.[119]

Spanish law, custom, and tradition were transferred to America and came to govern the position of the Negro slave. It is interesting to note that a large body of new law was developed for the treatment of the Indians in America, whereas the Negro's position was covered by isolated *cedulas* dealing with special problems. It was not until 1789 that a formal

---

[115] *Las Siete Partidas*, Ley XIII, tit. xvi, part. 3.
[116] Ibid., Ley XXI, tit. v, part. 6.
[117] Ibid., Ley VII, tit. xvi, part. 6.
[118] Ibid., Ley XXIII, tit. iii, part. 6.
[119] Ibid., Ley IX, tit. viii, part. 7.

code dealing with the Negro slave was promulgated.[120] But this new code, as recognized by the preamble itself, is merely a summary of the ancient and traditional law. Saco[121] says of it that it merely repeats in amplified form "our ancient laws," and the practice recommended is "very usual in our dominions of the Indies."

This body of law, containing the legal tradition of the Spanish people and also influenced by the Catholic doctrine of the equality of all men in the sight of God, was biased in favor of freedom and opened the gates to manumission when slavery was transferred to the New World. The law in Spanish and Portuguese America facilitated manumission, the tax-gatherer did not oppose it,[122] and the church ranked it among the works singularly agreeable to God. A hundred social devices narrowed the gap between bondage and liberty, encouraged the master to release his

---

[120] *Real Cedula de Su Magestad sobre la Educacion, Trato, y Ocupaciones de los Esclavos, en Todos sus Dominios de Indias, e Islas Filipinas, Baxo las Reglas que Se Expresan.* This law has been reprinted several times, most recently in an article by Raúl Carrancá y Trujillo in *Revista de Historia de America,* Numero 3 (Mexico, September 1938), pp. 50–9.

[121] José Antonio Saco, *Historia de la Esclavitud de la Raza Africana en el Nuevo Mundo y en especial en los Países Américo-Hispanos* (Havana: Cultural, s. a.; 1938), Tomo III, pp. 265–6.

[122] "In the Cuban market freedom was the only commodity which could be bought untaxed; every negro against whom no one had proved a claim of servitude was deemed free. . . ." William Law Mathieson, op. cit., pp. 37–8.

slave, and the ɒondsman to achieve freedom on his own account. From the sixteenth to the nineteenth century, slaves in Brazil, by reimbursing the original purchase price, could compel their masters to free them.[123] In Cuba and in Mexico the price might be fixed at the request of the Negro, and the slave was freed even if he cost "triple of the sum." [124] The right to have his price declared aided the Negro in seeking a new master, and the owner was required to transfer him to another.[125]

The law further permitted the slave to free himself by installments, and this became a widely spread custom, especially in Cuba.[126] A slave worth six hundred dollars could buy himself out in twenty-four installments of twenty-five dollars each, and with every payment he acquired one twenty-fourth of his own freedom. Thus, when he had paid fifty dollars, he owned one twelfth of himself.[127] On delivering his first installment, he could move from his master's

---

[123] Sir Harry Johnston, op. cit., p. 89. D. P. Kidder and J. C. Fletcher: *Brazil and the Brazilians* (New York: Childs and Peterson; 1857), p. 133.

[124] Alexander Humboldt: *Political Essay on the Kingdom of New Spain*, translated by John Black (New York: I. Riley; 1811), Vol. I, p. 181.

[125] Richard Henry Dana, Jr.: *To Cuba and Back* (Boston: Tichnor and Fields; 1859), p. 249.

[126] Fernando Ortiz: *Los Negros Esclavos* (Havana, 1916), p. 313.

[127] Alexander Humboldt: *The Island of Cuba*, op. cit., p. 211.

house,[128] and thereafter pay interest on the remaining sum, thus acquiring a position not materially different in effect from that of a man in debt who had specific monetary obligations. There seem to have been many instances of slaves paying out all of the installments due on their purchase price except the last fifty or one hundred dollars, and on these paying one half a real per day for every fifty pesos. The advantage in this arrangement apparently lay in the fact that a Negro, thus partially a slave, could escape the payment of taxes on his property and be free from military service.[129]

In effect, slavery under both law and custom had, for all practical purposes, become a contractual arrangement between the master and his bondsman. There may have been no written contract between the two parties, but the state behaved, in effect, as if such a contract did exist, and used its powers to enforce it. This presumed contract was of a strictly limited liability on the part of the slave, and the state, by employing the officially provided protector of slaves, could and did define the financial obligation of the slave to his master in each specific instance as it arose. Slavery had thus from a very early date, at least in so far as the practice was concerned, moved from a "status," or "caste," "by law of nature," or because of "innate inferiority," or because of the "just

---

[128] Fernando Ortiz, op. cit., p. 317.
[129] Ibid., p. 315.

judgment and provision of holy script," to become a mere matter of an available sum of money for redemption. Slavery had become a matter of financial competence on the part of the slave, and by that fact lost a great part of the degrading imputation that attached to slavery where it was looked upon as evidence of moral or biological inferiority. Slavery could be wiped out by a fixed purchase price, and therefore the taint of slavery proved neither very deep nor indelible.

In addition to making freedom something obtainable for money, which the slave had the right to acquire and possess, the state made manumission possible for a number of other reasons. A Negro could be freed if unduly punished by his master.[180] He was at liberty to marry a free non-slave (and the master could not legally interfere), and as under the law the children followed the mother, a slave's children born of a free mother were also free.[181] Slaves in Brazil who joined the army to fight in the Paraguayan war were freed by decree on November 6, 1866, and some twenty thousand Negroes were thus liberated.[182]

In the wars of independence many thousands of slaves in Venezuela and Colombia were freed by Bolívar and enlisted in the army of liberation. In Ar-

---

[180] Alexander Humboldt: *Political Essay*, op. cit., p. 181.

[181] Henry Koster: *Travels in Brazil* (Philadelphia: M. Carey & Son; 1817), Vol. II, p. 202. Fernando Ortiz, op. cit., p. 337.

[182] Percy Alvin Martin, op. cit., p. 174.

gentina perhaps as many as a third of San Martín's host that crossed the Andes was composed of freed Negroes. And, finally, as early as 1733, by a special *cedula* repeated twice later, slaves escaping to Cuba from other West Indian islands because they wished to embrace the Catholic religion could be neither returned to their masters, nor sold, nor given in slavery to any other person.[133]

But significant and varied as were these provisions of the law in the Spanish and Portuguese colonies, they were less important in the long run than the social arrangements and expectancies that prevailed. It was permissible for a slave child in Brazil to be freed at the baptismal font by an offer of twenty milreis,[134] and in Cuba for twenty-five dollars.[135] A female slave could seek a godfather for her baby in some respectable person, hoping that the moral obligation imposed upon the godfather would lead to freeing the child. It was both a meritorious and a pious deed to accept such a responsibility and to fulfill its implicit commitments, and it bestowed distinction upon him who accepted them.[136] In the mining regions of Minas Geraes a slave who found a seventeen and a half carat diamond was crowned with a floral wreath, dressed

---

[133] Fernando Ortiz, op. cit., p. 351.

[134] Robert Southey: *History of Brazil* (London, 1819), Part III, p. 784.

[135] William Law Mathieson, op. cit., p. 37.

[136] Henry Koster, op. cit., p. 195.

in a white suit, carried on the shoulders of fellow slaves to the presence of his master, and freed and allowed to work for himself.[137] A parent having ten children could claim freedom, whether male or female.

The freeing of one's slaves was an honorific tradition, and men fulfilled it on numerous occasions. Favorite wet nurses were often freed; slaves were manumitted on happy occasions in the family — a birth of a first son, or the marriage of one of the master's children. In fact, the excuses and the occasions were numerous — the passing of an examination in school by the young master, a family festival, a national holiday, and, of course, by will upon the death of the master.[138] A cataloguing of the occasions for manumission in such a country as Brazil might almost lead to wonder at the persistence of slavery; but as I have pointed out above, the importations of slaves were large and continuous in Brazil all through the colonial period and late into the nineteenth century.

Opportunities for escape from slavery were further facilitated by the system of labor that prevailed in many places, particularly in cities. Slaves were often encouraged to hire themselves out and bring their masters a fixed part of their wages, keeping the rest. Skilled artisans, masons, carpenters, blacksmiths,

---

[137] John Mawe: *Travels in the Interior of Brazil* (London: Longman, Hurst, Rees, Orme & Brown; 1812), p. 318.

[138] Percy Alvin Martin, op. cit., p. 170.

wheelwrights, tailors, and musicians were special gainers from the arrangement.[139] But even ordinary laborers were allowed to organize themselves in gangs, *gente de Ganho,* as they were called. Preceded by a leader, who would guide them in a rhythmic chant, they would offer their services as carriers on the wharves of the city or to do any heavy work that came to hand. The description of these chanting gangs of Negro slaves in the city of Rio, carrying bags of coffee on their heads, their sweating bodies stripped to the waist, marching in rhythm to their own song, is like nothing else in social history:

. . . the rapid lope and monotonous grunt of the coffee-bag carriers, their naked bodies reeking with oily sweat; the jingling and drumming of the tin rattles or gourds borne by the leaders of gangs, transporting on their heads all manner of articles — chairs, tables, sofas, and bedsteads, the entire furniture of a household; the dull recitative, followed by the loud chorus, with which they move along; the laborious cry of others, tugging and hauling and pushing over the rough pavements heavily laden trucks and carts, an overload for an equal number of mules or horses, all crowd on the observation. Others, both male and female, more favored in their occupation, are seen as peddlers, carrying in the same manner, trunks and boxes of tin, containing various merchandise; glass cases filled with fancy articles and jewelry; trays with cakes and confectionery; and baskets with fruit, flowers and birds. And yet again others of the same color and race, more fortunate still, in being free — the street-

---

[139] Fernando Ortiz, op. cit., p. 318.

vendor, the mechanic, the tradesman, the soldier; the merchant and the priest in his frock.[140]

But the slave in this procession had his wages for himself after paying the master his share. Individual persons in Rio, otherwise poor, would make their living from the owning of one or more of these male or female slaves, whom they permitted to hire themselves out.[141] Women often hired themselves out as wet nurses, and both male and female slaves peddled a thousand wares through the streets.

Slaves of both sexes cry wares through every street. Vegetables, flowers, fruits, edible roots, fowls, eggs, and every rural product, cakes, pies, rusks, doces, confectionery, "heavenly bacon," etc., pass your windows continually. Your cook wants a skillet, and, hark! the signal of a pedestrian copper-smith is heard; his bell is a stew-pan, and the clapper a hammer. A water-pot is shattered; in half an hour a meringue-merchant approaches. You wish to replenish your table-furniture with fresh sets of knives, new-fashioned tumblers, decanters, and plates, and, peradventure, a cruet, with a few articles of silver. Well, you need not want them long. If cases of cutlery, of glassware, china, and silver have not already passed the door, they will appear anon. So of every article of female apparel, from silk dress or shawl to a handkerchief and a paper of pins. Shoes, bonnets, ready trimmed, fancy jewelry, toy-books for children, novels for young folks, and works of devotion for the devout; "Art of Dancing" for the awkward; "School of Good Dress" for the young;

---

[140] C. S. Stewart: *Brazil and La Plata: the Personal Record of a Cruise* (New York: G. P. Putnam & Co.; 1856), p. 72.

[141] Rev. R. Walsh: *Notices of Brazil*, Vol. II, p. 20.

"Manual of Politeness" for boors; "Young Ladies' Oracle"; "Language of Flowers"; "Holy Reliquaries"; "Miracles of Saints," and "A Sermon in Honor of Bacchus" — these things, and a thousand others, are hawked about daily.[142]

With all its cruelty, abuse, hardship, and inhumanity, the atmosphere in Brazil and in the Spanish-American countries made for manumission. Even in the rural regions individuals were allowed to sell the products from their own plots, given them to work for themselves, and to save their money toward the day of freedom. In Cuba, one writer notes, the raising of pigs by slaves provided a ready source of the sums accumulated for such a purpose.[143] It should be further noticed that, in addition to their Sundays, the Negroes in Brazil had many holidays, amounting all together to eighty-four days a year, which they could use for their own purposes, and for garnering such funds as their immediate skill and opportunities made possible. The purchase of one's freedom was so accepted a tradition among the Negroes that many a Negro bought the freedom of his wife and children while he himself continued laboring as a slave, and among the freed Negroes societies were organized for pooling resources and collecting funds for the freeing of their brethren still in bondage.[144]

---

[142] Thomas Ewbank, op. cit., pp. 92–3.

[143] Rev. Abiel Abbot: *Letters Written in the Interior of Cuba* (Boston: Bowles and Dearborn; 1829), p. 97.

[144] Arthur Ramos: *The Negro in Brazil*, translated from the Portuguese by Richard Pattee (Washington, D.C., 1939), p. 70.

These many provisions favoring manumission were strongly influenced by the church. Without interfering with the institution of slavery where the domestic law accepted it, the church early condemned the slave trade and prohibited Catholics from taking part in it. The prohibition was not effective, though it in some measure may have influenced the Spaniards to a rather limited participation in the trade as such. The slave trade had been condemned by Pius II on October 7, 1462, by Paul III on May 29, 1537, by Urban VIII on April 2, 1639, by Benedict XIV on December 20, 1741, and finally by Gregory XVI on December 3, 1839. The grounds of the condemnation were that innocent and free persons were illegally and by force captured and sold into slavery, that rapine, cruelty, and war were stimulated in the search for human beings to be sold at a profit.[145] The Franciscan Father Thomas Mercado had condemned the slave trade in the strongest terms in the year 1587, on the grounds that it fostered two thousand falsehoods, a thousand robberies, and a thousand deceptions. But the church did not interfere with the customary institution where it derived from known practices in a given community, such as born slaves, slaves taken in a just war, or those who had sold themselves or had been condemned by a legitimate court.

The presumption against the slave trade was that it forced people into slavery outside the law and

---

[145] José Antonio Saco, op. cit., Tomo III, pp. 64–6.

against their will. More important in the long run than the condemnation of the slave trade proved the church's insistence that slave and master were equal in the sight of God. Whatever the formal relations between slave and master, they must both recognize their relationship to each other as moral human beings and as brothers in Christ. The master had an obligation to protect the spiritual integrity of the slave, to teach him the Christian religion, to help him achieve the privileges of the sacraments, to guide him into living a good life, and to protect him from mortal sin. The slave had a right to become a Christian, to be baptized, and to be considered a member of the Christian community. Baptism was considered his entrance into the community, and until he was sufficiently instructed to be able to receive it, he was looked upon as out of the community and as something less than human.[146]

From the very beginning the Catholic churches in America insisted that masters bring their slaves to church to learn the doctrine and participate in the communion. The assembled bishops in Mexico in the year 1555 urged all Spaniards to send the Indians, and especially the Negroes, to church; [147] similarly in Cuba in 1680.[148]

---

[146] Henry Koster, op. cit., p. 199.

[147] *Concilios Provinciales, Primero y Segundo, Mexico, En los Años de 1555 y 1565* (Mexico, 1769), Concilio primero, Cap. III, p. 44.

[148] José Antonio Saco, op. cit., Tomo I, pp. 165–7.

In fact, Negroes were baptized in Angola [149] before leaving for their Atlantic journey to Brazil. Upon arrival they were instructed in the doctrine, and as evidence of their baptism carried about their necks a mark of the royal crown. As a Catholic the slave was married in the church, and the banns were regularly published.[150] It gave the slave's family a moral and religious character unknown in other American slave systems. It became part of the ordinary routine on the slave plantations for the master and slaves to attend church on Sundays, and regularly before retiring at night the slaves gathered before the master's house to receive his blessings.[151] If married by the church, they could not be separated by the master. Religious fraternities sprang up among the slaves. These were often influential and honorific institutions, with regularly elected officers, and funds for the celebration of religious holidays subscribed to by the slaves out of their own meager savings. In Brazil the slaves adopted the Lady of the Rosary as their own special patroness, sometimes painting her black. In a measure these religious fraternities emulated those of the whites, if they did not compete with them, and the slaves found a source of pride in becoming members,

---

[149] Henry Koster, op. cit., p. 198.

[150] Ibid., p. 202.

[151] Alfred R. Wallace: *A Narrative of Travels on the Amazon and Rio Negro* (London: Reeve & Co.; 1853), p. 92.

and honor in serving one of these religious fraternities as an official.[152]

If the Latin-American environment was favorable to freedom, the British and American were hostile.[153] Legal obstacles were placed in the way of manumission, and it was discouraged in every other manner. The presumption was in favor of slavery.[154] A Negro who could not prove that he was free was presumed to be a runaway slave and was advertised as such; if no claimant appeared, he was sold at public auction for the public benefit.[155] In Demerara no slave could be manumitted without the consent of the Governor and Council. In most of the British colonies heavy taxes

---

[152] Robert Southey, op. cit., p. 784.

[153] There were, briefly speaking, three slave systems in the Western Hemisphere. The British, American, Dutch, and Danish were at one extreme, and the Spanish and Portuguese at the other. In between these two fell the French. The first of these groups is characterized by the fact that they had no effective slave tradition, no slave law, and that their religious institutions were little concerned about the Negro. At the other extreme there were both a slave law and a belief that the spiritual personality of the slave transcended his slave status. In between them the French suffered from the lack of a slave tradition and slave law, but did have the same religious principles as the Spaniards and Portuguese. If one were forced to arrange these systems of slavery in order of severity, the Dutch would seem to stand as the hardest, the Portuguese as the mildest, and the French, in between, as having elements of both.

[154] William Law Mathieson, op. cit., pp. 38–40.

[155] Ibid., pp. 38–40.

had been imposed on manumission, and as late as
1802 a law was passed in the Northern Leeward Islands requiring the owner who would register his
slave for manumission to pay five hundred pounds
into the public treasury,[156] and this sum had to be provided in his will if it made provision for the liberation
of the slave. The slave could not be freed without
the master's consent, even if the full price of the slave
was offered. In the fear of an increase of freemen,
Barbados, in 1801, passed a law taxing the manumission of a female slave much more heavily than a male.
St. Christopher, which taxed manumission for the
first time in 1802, declared it to be a "great inconven-
ience . . . that [the number of] free Negroes and
. . . free persons of color was augmented" by releas-
ing slaves from bondage, and provided that a slave
who had been released by his master, but not formally
enfranchised, should be "publicly sold at vendue." [157]

In the southern part of the United States the position of the slave was closely similar to that in the
British West Indies. What is important to note is the
tendency to identify the Negro with the slave. The
mere fact of being a Negro was presumptive of a
slave status. South Carolina in 1740 (similarly
Georgia and Mississippi) provided that "all negroes,
Indians (those now free excepted) . . . mulattoes,
or mestizos, who are or shall hereafter be in the prov-

---

[156] Sir Harry Johnston, op. cit., p. 231.
[157] William Law Mathieson, op. cit., pp. 38–40.

ince, and all their issue and offspring, born or to be born, shall be and they are hereby declared to be and remain forever hereafter absolute slaves and shall follow the condition of the mother." [158] Equally striking is an early law of Maryland, dating from 1663: "All negroes or other slaves within the province, all negroes to be hereafter imported, shall serve *durante vita*"; and their children were to follow the condition of the father. Significantly the same law said: "That whatsoever freeborn women (English) shall intermarry with any slave . . . shall serve the master of such slave during the life of her husband; all the issue of such freeborn women, so married, shall be slave as their fathers were." [159] A free Negro in South Carolina (1740) harboring a runaway slave, or charged "with any criminal matter," upon inability to pay the fine and court charges was to be sold "at public auction." [160] The same state provided that an emancipated Negro set free otherwise than according to the act of 1800 could be seized and kept as a slave by "any person whatsoever."

The Negro was a slave, and the pressure seemed, in a number of states, anyway, to keep him one, or to reduce him to slavery if free. In Virginia an emanci-

---

[158] George M. Stroud: *A Sketch of the Laws Relating to Slavery in the Several States of the United States of America* (2nd edition, Philadelphia: H. Longstreth; 1856), pp. 60–1.

[159] Ibid., p. 14.

[160] Ibid., p. 24.

pated slave who had not left the state in the twelve
months after being manumitted could be sold by the
overseer of the poor "for the benefit of the Literary
Fund"; [161] similarly in North Carolina. In Florida
a free mulatto or Negro could be made a slave for the
smallest debt executed against him. In Mississippi
any Negro or mulatto not being able to show himself
a free man could be sold by the court as a slave. In
Maryland (1717) any free Negro or mulatto, man or
woman, intermarrying with a white person became
a slave for life.[162] Because the Negroes were brought
in as slaves, the black color raised the presumption of
slavery, which was generally extended to mulattoes,
and in many states this presumption was enunciated
by statute, putting on them the onus of proving that
they were free. In Virginia and Kentucky one-fourth
Negro blood constituted a presumption of slavery,
and all children born of slave mothers were slaves.[163]

Under the British West Indian and United States
laws the Negro slave could not hope for self-redemp-
tion by purchase, and as slavery was assumed to be
perpetual, there was only one route to freedom —
manumission. But this route, if not entirely blocked,
was made difficult by numerous impediments. The

---

[161] Quoted in George M. Stroud, op. cit., p. 27.

[162] Ibid., pp. 27–30.

[163] Thomas R. R. Cobb: *An Inquiry into the Law of Negro
Slavery in the United States of America* (Philadelphia and Savannah, 1858), p. 238.

bias in favor of keeping the Negro in servitude contrasts with the other slave systems here under consideration, describes the explicit and the implicit test of the two systems, and foreshadows their ultimate outcome. For the attitude toward manumission is the crucial element in slavery; it implies the judgment of the moral status of the slave, and foreshadows his role in case of freedom.

Just as the favoring of manumission is perhaps the most characteristic and significant feature of the Latin-American slave system, so opposition to manumission and denial of opportunities for it are the primary aspect of slavery in the British West Indies and in the United States. The frequency and ease of manumission, more than any other factor, influence the character and ultimate outcome of the two slave systems in this hemisphere. For the ease of manumission bespeaks, even if only implicitly, a friendly attitude toward the person whose freedom is thus made possible and encouraged, just as the systematic obstruction of manumission implies a complete, if unconscious, attitude of hostility to those whose freedom is opposed or denied. And these contrasting attitudes toward manumission work themselves out in a hundred small, perhaps unnoticed, but significant details in the treatment of the Negro, both as a slave and when freed. Either policy reveals the bent of the system, and casts ahead of itself the long-run consequence of immediate practice and attitude.

In the United States, "in every slaveholding state . . . restrictions . . . have been placed upon the manumission of Negro slaves. . . . In several of the states domestic manumission, that is, manumission to take effect within the state is prohibited." [164] In Mississippi, Alabama, and Maryland manumission by will was void. Manumission could not be effected to the prejudice of creditors, and if the estate proved insolvent, manumission by will was of no effect. [165] In states like Mississippi, Virginia, and Kentucky, where a widow was entitled to one third of her deceased husband's estate, slaves emancipated by will could be held for the satisfaction of the widow's rights. [166] In South Carolina, Georgia, Alabama, and Mississippi manumission was valid only with the consent of the state legislature. A fine of two hundred dollars was visited upon the master in Georgia (1801) for attempting to manumit a slave without previous consent of the legislature, and the slave continued in bondage as before. In 1818 this same state imposed a fine of one thousand dollars on anyone giving effect to a last will and testament freeing a slave or permitting him to work for himself beyond the control of a master. In North Carolina (1836–7) a surety of one thousand dollars was required before manumission for the guarantee of the freed slave's good behavior, and

---

[164] Thomas R. R. Cobb, op. cit., pp. 287, 290.

[165] Ibid., pp. 296, 298.

[166] George M. Stroud, op. cit., p. 231.

the freed slave had to leave the state within ninety days, never to return. Tennessee (1801) required a bond, the consent of the court, and immediate departure from the state; whereas in Mississippi (1822) there had to be an instrument in writing proving to the General Assembly that the slave had performed a meritorious deed, and then a special act sanctioning the manumission in question.[167] The laws of Virginia effecting emancipation had undergone many changes.

In Virginia, in 1691, it was provided that a Negro could not be set free unless "pay for the transportation of such negro" out of the "country" within six months be provided.[168] In 1723 an act provided that a Negro could be set free only by the action of the Governor and Council, and only for some "meritorious service." In 1805 Virginia prohibited emancipation unless the Negro left the state.[169] In 1824 the Virginia courts ruled that the freeing of a mother by will after she reached a certain age did not apply to her children born after the date of the will.[170] Many similar statutes were passed in other states.

The slave had no protector to appeal to, and the master had, in some instances, exceeding power over

---

[167] Ibid., pp. 219–36.

[168] Helen Tunnicliff Catterall: *Judicial Cases Concerning American Slavery and the Negro*, with additions by James J. Hayden (5 vols., Washington, D. C.: Carnegie Institution of Washington; 1926–1937), Vol. I, p. 72.

[169] Ibid., p. 73.

[170] Ibid., p. 74.

him. An early Jamaican statute provided: "If any
slave by punishment from his owner for running
away, or other offence, suffer in life or limb, none
shall be liable to the law for the same; but whoever
shall kill a slave out of willfulness, wantonness, or
bloody-mindedness, shall suffer three months' im-
prisonment and pay £50 to the owner of the slave." [171]
Thus willful murder had been reduced to a misde-
meanor if committed on a slave. But it is more surprising that if the murder was committed by an indentured
servant, he too could expiate the murder by thirty-
nine lashes and four years' service.[172] Tennessee provided that the law defining the killing of a slave as
murder should not apply "to any person killing a slave
. . . in the act of resistance . . . or dying under
moderate correction." [173] The Georgia constitution
safeguards against the charge of murder if the "death
should happen by accident in giving such slave moderate correction." [174] In South Carolina the act of 1740
provided that willful murder of a slave should cost

---

[171] Charles Leslie, op. cit., p. 234. *The Laws of Jamaica,
Passed by the Assembly and Confirmed by His Majesty, in Council April 17, 1684* (London, 1684). In 1696 willful killing of a
slave on the second offense was to be considered as murder and punishable as such without benefit of clergy. *Acts of Jamaica 1681–
1737* (London, 1738), p. 8. In 1717 anyone ordering a slave dis-
membered was to pay £100 (ibid., p. 160).

[172] Charles Leslie, op. cit., p. 234.

[173] George M. Stroud, op. cit., pp. 60–1.

[174] Art. 4, par. 12, in ibid., p. 61.

the perpetrator "seven hundred pounds current money," and this law, which remained on the statute books till 1821, further provided that if the murder occurred "on sudden heat and passion," it should cost him only £350.[175] But such minor punishments as willfully cutting out the tongue, putting out the eye, castrating, scalding, and similar offenses would, according to the above law, involve the culprit in a cost of merely "one hundred pounds of current money." [176]

Where laws existed protecting the slave against unusual punishment, they were difficult to enforce because he was denied the right to testify in the courts. In the United States, according to Cobb,[177] the rule that slaves could not testify for or against free white persons was enforced without exception; most of the states prohibited such testimony by express statute, others by custom and decision of the courts. In Illinois and Iowa this prohibition extended to free persons of color or emancipated slaves. The testimony of any Negro or mulatto, free or bond, was accepted in Virginia only in cases where free Negroes and mulattoes were parties, and in no other case whatsoever.[178] Similar laws were enacted in most of the Southern states.

---

[175] Ibid., p. 64.
[176] Ibid., p. 66.
[177] Thomas R. R. Cobb, op. cit., p. 230.
[178] "Revised Code 422," quoted in George M. Stroud, op. cit., p. 300.

The slave had no protector to appeal to, and he could not have his price specified for purposes of redemption and was not allowed to accumulate property to buy his freedom. The slave could acquire no property, and if any property came to him, it would belong to his master; [179] and, being incapable of acquiring property, he could not convey it or give it away. The laws on this point are numerous. In Lousiana, "all that a slave possesses belongs to his master," [180] and he "cannot dispose or receive by donation." In South Carolina, "Slaves cannot take by descent or purchase"; in North Carolina, "Slaves cannot take by sale, or device, or descent." As one court put it, "Our slaves can do nothing in their own right, can hold no property, can neither buy, sell, barter, nor dispose of anything without express permission of master or overseer. . . ." [181] But other states went further — they denied the right of the slave to own property, even with the consent of the master. Under the act of 1740 South Carolina made it illegal for any slave to "raise and breed for the benefit of such slave, any horses, mares, cattle, sheep, or hogs under pain of forfeiture of all such goods, etc." [182] Georgia punished the master by a fine of thirty dollars "for every weekly

---

[179] Thomas R. R. Cobb, op. cit., p. 238.
[180] William Goodell: *The American Slave Code* (New York, 1853), p. 90.
[181] Ibid., p. 52.
[182] Ibid., pp. 97–100.

offence" if he permitted his slave to hire himself out
to another for his own benefit.[183] Similar laws were
enacted in Kentucky, Tennessee, Virginia, and Mis-
souri. In Mississippi a slave could not raise cotton for
his own use, and the master permitting it was fined
fifty dollars. The laws further restricted the hiring
out of slaves to others; Virginia in 1819 made it permissible to sell a slave for hiring himself out.[184]

The marriage contract having no validity, none of
its consequences followed. While in a state of slavery,
marriage, even with the master's consent, produced
no civil effect.[185] The question of marriage of the
slave troubled the conscience of good people, and they
attempted to meet the issue posed by the absolute
power of separation by the master.

In 1835, the following query relating to slaves was pro-
pounded to the Savannah River Baptist Association of ministers: Whether, in case of involuntary separation of such a
character as to preclude all further intercourse, the parties
may be allowed to marry again?

ANSWER. — That such separation, among persons situated
as our slaves are, is, civilly, a separation by death, and they

---

[183] Ibid., p. 98.

[184] Ibid., p. 101. The states having slaves were so numerous,
the changes in the law so frequent, and their enforcement so
uneven at different times that it is impossible to describe every
detail in all of its variations. A special treatise on the law and practice for every state would be required. But even if the details vary,
in all of the Southern states the tendency to discourage manumission and to identify the freedman with the slave is clear.

[185] Ibid., p. 107.

believe that, in the sight of God, it would be so viewed. To
forbid second marriage in such cases, would be to expose the
parties not only to greater hardships and stronger temptations,
but to *church censure* for acting in *obedience to their masters,*
who cannot be expected to acquiesce in a regulation at vari-
ance with justice to the slaves, and to the spirit of that com-
mand which regulates marriage between Christians. *The
slaves are not free agents,* and a dissolution by death is not
more entirely without their consent and beyond their control than by such separation.[186]

In 1779 North Carolina prohibited the ownership
of animals by slaves. Mississippi prohibited a master
from allowing his slave to trade like a freeman, and
Maryland from permitting him to keep "stock of any
description," nor could he acquire money beyond his
wages for the purchase of the freedom of his children.[187]

There was no custom of freeing the children at the
baptismal font for a nominal price, there was nothing
known of the moral role of the godfather for the slave
child, and the slave family had no status either in
law or in public recognition.

The law recognized no marriage relation between
slaves.[188] There followed no inheritance of blood even
after emancipation,[189] and spouses might be witnesses
against each other. It was part of the record that "A

---

[186] Quoted in William Goodell, op. cit., p. 109.
[187] George M. Stroud, op. cit., p. 81.
[188] Thomas R. R. Cobb, op. cit., p. 243.
[189] Ibid., p. 245.

slave never has maintained an action against the violator of his bed. A slave is not admonished for incontinence, or punished for fornication or adultery; never prosecuted for bigamy, or petty treason, for killing a husband being a slave, any more than admitted to an appeal for murder." [190]

Under the law of most of the Southern states, there was no regard for the Negro family, no question of the right of the owner to sell his slaves separately, and no limitation upon separating husband and wife, or child from its mother. That this was so may be seen from the following advertisements:

NEGROES FOR SALE. — A negro woman, 24 years of age, and her two children, one eight and the other three years old. Said negroes will be sold SEPARATELY or together, *as desired.* The woman is a good seamstress. She will be sold low for cash, or EXCHANGED FOR GROCERIES.
For terms, apply to MATTHEW BLISS & Co., 1 Front Levee
[*New Orleans Bee*]

I WILL GIVE THE HIGHEST CASH PRICE for likely Negroes, from 10 to 25 years of age.
GEORGE KEPHART
[*Alexandria* (D. C.) *Gazette*]

ONE HUNDRED AND TWENTY NEGROES FOR SALE. — The subscriber has *just arrived from Petersburg, Virginia,* with one hundred and twenty *likely young negroes* of both sexes and every description, which he offers for sale on the most

---

[190] "Opinion of Daniel Dulany, Esq., Attorney General of Maryland," Maryland Reports, 561, 563; quoted in George M. Stroud, op. cit., p. 99.

reasonable terms. The lot now on hand consists of plough-boys, several likely and well-qualified house servants of both sexes, *several women with children, small girls* suitable for nurses, and SEVERAL SMALL BOYS WITHOUT THEIR MOTH-ERS. Planters and *traders* are earnestly requested to give the subscriber a call previously to making purchases *elsewhere*, as he is enabled to sell as cheap or cheaper than can be sold by *any other person in the trade.*

BENJAMIN DAVIS
(Hamburg, S. C., September 28, 1838)[191]

But even more convincing than the advertisements is the following record compiled by Frederic C. Bancroft from four cargoes of Negroes shipped to New Orleans in 1834 and 1835:

Of the four cargoes making a total of 646 slaves, 396 were apparently owned by Franklin & Armfield. Among these there were only two full families: the fathers were 21 and 22 years of age, the mothers 19 and 20, and the children 1 and 1½. There were 20 husbandless mothers with 33 children, of whom one was 2 weeks old, 4 others were less than 1 year old, 19 were from 1 to 4 years old, and 9 were from 5 to 12 years of age. The remaining 337 were single and may be grouped thus:

5	were from	6 to	9	years old,	both	inclusive	
68	" "	10 "	15	"	"	"	"
145	" "	16 "	21	"	"	"	"
101	" "	22 "	30	"	"	"	"
9	" "	31 "	39	"	"	"	"
8	" "	40 "	50	"	"	"	"
1	above	50,	a man of 60.				

---

[191] William Goodell, op. cit., pp. 54–5.

93 per cent of these 337 were from 10 to 30 years of age.[192]

Under the law a slave could not acquire property by earning it, by gift, or by inheritance. Not having any property, he could make no will, and could not take by descent, "there being in him no inheritable blood." [193] In South Carolina slaves were described as "chattels personal . . . to all intents, constructions and purposes whatsoever." [194] In Louisiana the slave ". . . can do nothing, possess nothing, nor acquire anything but what must belong to his master." [195] In 1806, slaves were defined as real estate. The same principle ruled in Kentucky, but except for purposes of sale and execution of debts they were considered chattel. Most of the states defined slaves as chattel, and the laws of Maryland (1791) declared that "In case the personal property of a ward shall consist of specific articles such as slaves, working beasts, animals of any kind, stock furniture, plate, books, and so forth, the court . . . may at any time pass an order for the sale thereof." [196]

---

[192] Frederic C. Bancroft: *Slave-Trading in the Old South* (Baltimore: J. H. Furst Co.; 1931), p. 63.

[193] Thomas R. R. Cobb, op. cit., p. 238.

[194] William Goodell, op. cit., p. 23.

[195] Ibid.

[196] Ibid., p. 25, quoted from *A Practical Treatise of the Law of Slavery, being a Compilation of all the Decisions made on that subject, in the several Courts of the United States, and State Courts; with copious notes and references to the Statutes and*

In fact, the issue of female slaves in Maryland was considered part of the use, like that of other female animals. Court decisions are cited to the effect: "Suppose a brood mare is hired for five years, the foals belong to him who has a part of the use of the dam. The slave in Maryland, in this respect, is placed on no higher or different grounds." [197] In fact, the breeding of slaves for sale as if they were mere cattle came to be part of the recognized practice of slave and plantation-owners in some, perhaps most, of the slave states. The practice was of long standing, and seems to have antedated the abolition of the slave trade, for as far back as 1796 the following advertisement appeared in Charleston, South Carolina, offering fifty Negroes for sale:

. . . they are not Negroes selected out of a larger gang for the purpose of a sale, but are prime, their present Owner, with great trouble and expense, selected them out of many for several years past. They were purchased for stock and breeding Negroes, and to any Planter who particularly wanted them for that purpose, they are a very choice and desirable gang.[198]

In 1830 Virginia was credited with exporting 8,500 slaves annually. Thomas Jefferson Randolph said:

other authorities, systematically arranged, by Jacob D. Wheeler, Esq., Counsellor at Law (New York: Allan Pollock, Jr.; New Orleans: Benjamin Levy; 1837).

[197] William Goodell, op. cit., p. 20.

[198] Quoted in Frederic C. Bancroft, op. cit., p. 68, from U. B. Phillips (editor): *Plantation and Frontier*, Vol. II, p. 57.

"It is a practice, and an increasing practice in parts of Virginia, to rear slaves for market." [199] And the protagonist of slavery Thomas R. Dew, who became president of William and Mary College in 1836, said with pride that "Virginia is in fact a negro raising state for other states; she produces enough for her own supply, and six thousand for sale. . . . Virginians can raise [them] cheaper than they can buy; in fact, it [raising slaves] is one of their greatest sources of profit." [200]

This business had its implications and consequences. The Negro female was reduced to a breeding animal. "She [a girl about twenty years of age] . . . is very prolific in her generating qualities, and affords a rare opportunity for any person who wishes to raise a family of strong, healthy servants for . . . [his] own use. . . ." [201] The emphasis was upon raising children, for they could be sold at high prices. The records show that a child of four was worth $200, and another of six $150, [202] while there are indications of even higher prices. In 1857 children of four, five, and eight years were sold for $376, $400, and $785, respec-

---

[199] Quoted in Frederic C. Bancroft, op. cit., p. 69.

[200] Quoted in Frederic C. Bancroft, op. cit., p. 71, from Thomas R. Dew: *Review of the Debate in the Virginia Legislature of 1831 and 1832* (Richmond, 1832).

[201] Quoted by Bancroft, op. cit., p. 74, from the *Charleston Mercury* of May 16, 1838.

[202] Helen Tunnicliff Catterall, op. cit., Vol. I, p. 186.

tively.[203] The thing to do was to breed the Negro girls young. "A girl of seventeen that had borne two children was called a 'rattlin' good breeder' and commanded an extraordinary price." [204] The demise of the sanctity of marriage had become absolute, and the Negro had lost his moral personality. Legally he was a chattel under the law, and in practice an animal to be bred for the market. The logic of the situation worked itself out in time, but in the process the moral personality of the slave as a human being became completely obscured. It is no wonder that the right of redemption was seemingly nonexistent and the opportunity for manumission greatly restricted.

The contrast between the United States and British West Indian slave law, on the one hand, and the Spanish and Portuguese, on the other, was further heightened by the different role of the church in the life of the Negro. The slaves in the British West Indies were almost completely denied the privileges of Christianity. The plantation-owners opposed the preaching of the gospel on the grounds that it would interfere with the management of the slaves, make them recalcitrant, and put notions of rebellion and

[203] Quoted in Frederic C. Bancroft, op. cit., p. 79, note, from Weston: *Progress of Slavery*, pp. 116–7.

[204] Frederic C. Bancroft, op. cit., p. 82.

freedom into their minds. The argument that the Christian doctrine would make the slaves more obedient, and therefore more docile, found little response among the planters. More surprising than the attitude of the slave-owners is that of the church itself. It is little exaggeration to say, as does one writer on the West Indies, that "The English Church did not recognize them as baptisable human beings." [205] For in spite of the fact that the Society for the Propagation of the Gospel, organized in 1701, declared through the mouth of Bishop Fleetwood, in 1710, that the three hundred Negroes that it had inherited in Barbados had to be brought into the church, and "that if all the slaves in America and every island in those seas were to continue infidels forever, yet ours alone must yet be Christian," [206] the church remained indifferent to its responsibility.

The official church did little indeed for the hundreds and thousands of West Indian Negro slaves. The Episcopal church confined its own activities to the whites and left the Negroes to the dissident denominations. But even these came late upon the scene and found little opportunity to preach the gospel. As a general rule the missionary preachers were opposed and ridiculed; in some instances they were driven out. The Quakers seem to have come first to the island of

---

[205] Amos K. Fiske: *The West Indies*, p. 108.

[206] Quoted in the Hon. H. A. Wyndham: *The Atlantic and Slavery*, p. 235.

Barbados, but their efforts proved unfruitful, and it was not till the Moravians established their first settlements in Jamaica, in 1732, that the Protestant gospel found a voice among the slaves. By 1787 there were missionary stations, in addition to Jamaica, in Antigua, St. Christopher, and Barbados. But the opposition to the preaching of the gospel continued into the nineteenth century and beyond the passage of the act abolishing the slave trade in 1807.

This persistent refusal of baptism "touched the English conscience to the raw," [207] but custom, tradition, hostility, and fear on the part of the planters proved stronger than missionary zeal. As one writer puts it, "I sincerely believe and am well assured that the slaves being instructed would be less attentive to labor, less inclined to obey their overseers and other deputies, and would be more anxious and more easily enabled to throw off the yoke of slavery altogether." [208] In contrast to Spanish provisions, the law had set up no requirements for the religious training of the Negroes, and it was not till 1816 that the Assembly of Jamaica ordered the vestries to provide chapels, and the curates to attend on Sunday after-

---

[207] Charles Booth: *Zachary Macaulay* (London, 1934), p. 32.

[208] R. Bickell: *The West Indies as They Are* (London, 1825), p. 120. In 1696 the Assembly of Jamaica had suggested that owners and overseers "shall as much as in them lies, endeavor the instruction of their slaves in the principle of the Christian religion" and shall "do their best to fit them for baptism" (*Acts of Jamaica*, p. 80).

noons for the instruction of the Negroes, and on two days a week to visit the neighboring plantations for the same purpose. But action was slow and indifferent, and as late as 1820 no chapel had been built in spite of the fact that some ten or twelve curates had by then been appointed, although some chapels were built after that.

We thus see that it was only after the abolition of the slave trade, and when the very institution of slavery itself was on the verge of extinction in the British West Indies, that legal action favoring Christian teaching for the Negroes was adopted. The effect of all this upon the fortunes of the Negro was very serious. As he was not a Christian, marriage in his case was not considered a sacrament and was not encouraged. The wife had no legal status and the family, as such, was not a unit. Legally the British slaves could not be married, and the religious unions could be dissolved at any time. In the years 1821–5 one devoted missionary had married, in his own parish, 1,085 couples, and in some of the others the marriages in this period ranged from one to five,[209] and this in a slave population of over 300,000, while in most of the other British West Indies no marriages had ever taken place. Under an act of the British Parliament, slaves could be sold by the sheriff in the execution of all debts.[210] It was not uncommon to break up the

---

[209] William Law Mathieson, op. cit., p. 41.
[210] Bryan Edwards, op. cit., Vol. II, p. 366.

families of the slaves in the satisfaction of debts as well as taxes.

Nor can it be said that the church in the United States was completely unrestricted in preaching the gospel. A series of regulations governing the assembly of Negroes for worship before dawn or after dark seriously interfered with church gatherings; the outright prohibition of Negro preachers or official frowning upon them, the opposition to acquisition of literacy on the part of either slave or freed man, all combined to restrict the development of a Negro church. And the white church proved incompetent to preach the gospel to all the millions of American Negroes. In South Carolina, in 1800, it was prohibited for "any number" of Negroes, mulattoes, or mestizos, even in company with white persons, to meet together for mental instruction or religious worship "before sunrise or after sunset." [211] Similar laws prevailed in many states. In some instances, the church raised its voice in despair at the situation and acknowledged its inability to remedy it:

The Presbyterian Synod of South Carolina and Georgia, in 1833, published a statement in which they said of the slaves: "There are over TWO MILLIONS of human being in the condition of heathen, and some of them in a worse condition." "They may justly be considered the HEATHEN of this country, and will bear a comparison with heathen in any country in the world. *The negroes are destitute of the gospel, and ever will be under the present state of things.* In the vast

---

[211] William Goodell, op. cit., p. 329.

field extending from an entire State beyond the Potomac [i.e., Maryland] to the Sabine River [at that time our south-western boundary], and from the Atlantic to the Ohio, there are, to the best of our knowledge, *not twelve* men exclusively devoted to the religious instruction of the negroes. In the present state of feeling in the South, a ministry of their own color could neither be obtained NOR TOLERATED. But do not the negroes have access to the gospel through the stated ministry of the whites? We answer, NO. The negroes have no regular and efficient ministry: as a matter of course, no churches; neither is there sufficient room in the white churches for their accommodation. We know of but *five* churches in the slaveholding States, built expressly for their use. These are all in the State of Georgia. We may now inquire whether they enjoy the privileges of the gospel in their own houses, and on our plantations? Again we return a negative answer. They have no Bibles to read by their own firesides. They have no family altars; and when in affliction, sickness, or death, they have no minister to address to them the consolations of the gospel, nor to bury them with appropriate services.[212]

The Methodist church, which was the most active in evangelizing the Negro in Georgia, in 1860 had 25,859 communicants out of 462,198 Negro slaves.

The first Methodist mission was organized by the South Carolina Conference in 1809. By 1839 there were 3,864 members, when there were about 280,-000 Negroes, and in 1857 there were 8,114 Negro communicants.[213] The Baptist and Episcopal churches

---

[212] Cited in William Goodell, op. cit., pp. 334–5.

[213] Ralph Betts Flanders: *Plantation Slavery in Georgia* (Chapel Hill, 1933), p. 178.

were also active, though no records of their communicants are available. The general situation, however, is reflected by the comment of a minister writing in 1858, when he said there "are hundreds of wealthy persons in our cotton growing sections" who permitted their slaves to live "in the most profound ignorance of the simplest truths of Christianity." [214]

In spite of these criticisms of the church in the United States, it is still true that, at least after 1700, there was no such systematic opposition to teaching the Christian doctrine to the Negro slave as there was in the British West Indies. How the teachings of Christ were reconciled with the complete disregard of the family and moral status of the slave is a major mystery. But the record will show numerous instances of masters encouraging church attendance by their slaves, and the provision of opportunities for hearing the gospel preached by white and occasionally even by colored ministers. [215]

The contrast, therefore, between the Spanish and Portuguese slave systems on the one hand and that of the British and the United States was very marked, and not merely in their effect upon the slave, but even more significantly upon the place and moral status of the freed man. Under the influence of the law and religion, the social milieu in the Spanish and Portu-

---

[214] Ralph Betts Flanders, op. cit., p. 180.

[215] Gunnar Myrdal: *An American Dilemma* (New York, 1944), Vol. II, pp. 859–60.

guese colonies made easy room for the Negroes passing from slavery to freedom. The older Mediterranean tradition of the defense of the slave, combined
with the effect of Latin-American experience, had
prepared an environment into which the Negro freed
from slavery could fit without visible handicap. Slavery itself carried no taint. It was a misfortune that had
befallen a human being, and was in itself sufficiently
oppressive. The law and religion both frowned upon
any attempts to convert this into a means of further
oppression. A *Real Cedula*, dated November 14,
1693, and directed to the Captain General of Cuba,
expresses in the name of the King the following very
revealing sentiments:

That after privately calling the masters of these slaves, you
say to them in my name that they must not, for whatever
motive, rigorously tighten the wage they receive from their
slaves, for having been tried in other places, it has proved in-
convenient harming the souls of these people, which is a matter for grave scruples that, for their own conscience' sake,
the master must avoid. . . . And at the same time I com-
mand you that if at any time . . . [these masters] mistreat
them [the slaves] you will apply the necessary remedy. It is
not just to consent to, or permit any excess in this matter, for
their slavery is a sufficient sorrow without at the same time
suffering the distempered rigour of their masters. . . .[216]

---

[216] Quoted in José Antonio Saco, op. cit., Tomo II, pp. 169–
70. We may contrast this with the following by Abel P. Upshur,
Secretary of State of the United States, to Edward Everett, United
States Minister to Great Britain, Washington, September 28,
1843:

If the law was solicitous to protect the Negro slave against abuse and defended him as a human being, the church opened its doors to him as a Christian, and as early as the eighteenth century in Brazil there were not only Negro priests, but even black bishops. And in Brazil, anyway, the Negro clergy seem to "have been more reverent, better living, more earnest than the Portuguese clergy." [217] Many things had conspired to give the Negro in America a special place in the community. The fact that he had come with the conqueror, that in a measure he was part of the conquering host, that he was used by the whites as boss and foreman over Indians in Mexico, Venezuela, and other places, the fact that he, unlike the Indian, had learned the language of his masters and taken many of his habits and customs, all combined to identify him with the European community and make him part of it. In every instance the Negro participated with the whites in their wars on equal terms, and in some of them he achieved the prestige of a national

"No man who knows anything of his own nature can suppose it to be possible that two races of men, distinguished by external and ineffaceable marks obvious to every eye, who had held towards each other from time immemorial the relation of master and slave, could ever live together as equals, in the same country and under the same Government. If, therefore, slavery be abolished, the one or the other of the races must leave the country or be exterminated. This would be for the slaves, because they are the weaker party." From William R. Manning, op. cit., Vol. VII, p. 12.

[217] Sir Harry Johnston, op. cit., p. 90.

hero. Thus in Brazil one of the two national heroes, dating from early colonial wars against the Dutch, is Henrique Dias. In Brazil, too, the Negroes had established their reputation for physical courage and military prowess in their mighty defense of the Negro Republic of Palmares (1650–96), which required an army of six thousand men and many years to destroy. In the wars for independence the Negro was an important element, and in Cuba the Negroes provided a majority of the army in the long struggle against Spain.

It is not surprising, therefore, that the political and social environment in Latin America has proved different. Not only was the Negro encouraged to secure his freedom, but once he was free, no obstacles were placed to his incorporation into the community, in so far as his skills and abilities made that possible. In Brazil the Negroes had done all of the work during the colonial period. It was in their ranks that all of the skills, crafts, and arts were to be found, and it was from the ranks of the Negroes and mulattoes that some of the great artists, musicians, and sculptors were drawn. Rich planters in Brazil often educated their bright mulatto children and even sent them to Lisbon in pursuit of learning. Negro slaves were often specially educated in specific arts, and Koster [218] notes an instance of a planter who had trained up a private band of musicians by sending some of them to Rio

[218] Henry Koster, op. cit., p. 174.

and others to Lisbon. The ranks of the regular army were open to free Negroes and mulattoes, and special Negro regiments were common, sometimes with their own Negro officers, not merely in Brazil but in Cuba and during the revolution for independence in Venezuela.

A peculiar feature of the slave system in Brazil and in other areas was the large plantations belonging to different religious orders, like those of the Franciscans, the Dominicans, and the Society of Jesus. On these plantations the Negroes were especially well treated and protected, their moral and religious training was looked after, and they were almost never sold. In fact, the Negroes on these plantations considered themselves as belonging to the saint rather than to the friars who looked after them.[219]

Upon gaining their freedom, the Negroes and their children found openings in private and public employment and even in public office. And if the question of color was raised, it became evident that the office weighed more than the color, so that a mulatto captain was declared to be white. This happened even in cases of the nobility in Brazil. Where a Negro probably could not have found a place, a mulatto could; how could a member of the nobility be anything but white? [220] Free Negroes had the same rights before the law and were allowed to hold property and, from

---

[219] Henry Koster, op. cit., pp. 217–8.
[220] Hon. H. A. Wyndham, op. cit., p. 250.

the beginning, take part in public life. The Negro, in fact, had acquired a moral personality while slavery still flourished. For all of these rights were enjoyed by the Negro when slavery was still in effect, and when hundreds of thousands and in some instances millions of his fellow blacks were still suffering the evils of slavery.

Nothing said above must induce the reader to believe that slavery was anything but cruel. It was often brutal. The difference between the systems lies in the fact that in the Spanish and Portuguese colonies the cruelties and brutalities were against the law, that they were punishable, and that they were perhaps not so frequent as in the British West Indies and the North American colonies. But these abuses had a remedy at law, and the Negro had a means of escape legally, by compulsory sale if the price were offered, and by many other means. More important was the fact that the road was open to freedom, and, once free, the Negro enjoyed, on the whole, a legal status equal to that of any other subject of the King or to that of any other citizen of the state. And if the question of color was an issue, he could purchase "whiteness" for a specific price.

If we now contrast the position of the freed Negro and people of color in the British possessions with those we have just described, it will become evident that whereas freedom in one place meant moral status, in the other it meant almost the opposite. In the British West Indies the achievement of manumission merely involved a release from the obligation to serve a special master. It did not carry with it any new rights, or, as Edwards puts it, "the courts of law interpreted the act of manumission by the owner, as nothing more than an abandonment, or release of his own proper authority over the person of the slave, which did not, and could not, convey to the object of his bounty, the civil and political rights of a natural-born subject; and the same principle was applied to the issue of freed mothers, until after the third generation from the Negro ancestor." [221] In most of the islands freed Negroes or mulattoes could not give evidence in court against white persons or even against people of color. They were thus less protected than slaves, who had their master to defend them against abuse or maltreatment. They were not permitted to serve even as petty officers of public trust, as in parochial vestries, or as constables. They could not hold office in the black militia, they could not vote. By a law of 1762 in Jamaica, they were deprived of the right to inherit more than £2,000, unless born of lawful marriage. [222] It was not until 1796 that people of color were allowed to give evidence in court against whites. Freed Negroes could not be tried by jury and

---

[221] Bryan Edwards, op. cit., p. 217.
[222] "Laws of Jamaica," from John Henry Howard: *Laws of the British Colonies in the West Indies and Other Parts of America* (2 vols., London, 1827), Vol. II, p. 58.

were subject to the same procedure as slaves. Freed persons could not even testify against slaves till after 1748. It was not until 1824 that free Negroes were permitted to give evidence in the courts under oath. One slave-owner reports:

> The murder was committed in the presence of several Negroes; but Negroes are not allowed to give evidence, and as no free person was present, there are not only doubts whether the murderer will be punished, but whether he can even be put upon his trial.[223]

One of the difficulties in the situation was the fact that the Negroes, not being, as a general rule, members of the Christian church, were considered incapable of taking an oath and, being deprived of that privilege, were automatically eliminated from all responsibilities and opportunities wherein the taking of an oath was a prerequisite.

The position of the manumitted Negro, or even of the mulatto born of a free mother, was not propitious. The legal and social environment was discriminatory and hostile. The English community opposed manumission, feared the growth of free colored people, and reduced those few who had found a route to freedom to as nearly a servile state as possible. In the United States a very similar policy toward freedmen developed. An act of manumission was merely a withdrawal of the rights of the master. It did not confer

---

[223] M. G. Lewis: *Journal of a West India Proprietor, 1815–17*, p. 328.

citizenship upon the freedmen. That power rested with the state.[224] They were not privileged to bear arms, they had to have a guardian to stand in the relation of a patron to them, and in some instances they were denied the right to purchase slaves as property. They tended to be placed on the same footing as slaves in their contact with whites.

A free colored person could be enslaved for assisting a runaway slave, for being suspected as a slave by white witnesses and unable to prove the contrary, and for inability to pay a fine. Though free in the North, he could be enslaved by entering a slave state (Georgia or Maryland) or for marrying a slave. Mississippi, in 1831, required all free colored persons over sixteen and under sixty to leave the state in ninety days unless they could secure a certificate of good character from the county courts. A free colored man had his ears cut off for striking a white man in Maryland, and was denied trial by jury in South Carolina. In North Carolina he could not preach the gospel, nor trade out of the city where he resided. In South Carolina free Negro seamen arriving in port could be taken from the ship and imprisoned at the expense of the ship's master.[225] These restrictions placed the freedmen but little above the slaves in respect to civil privileges. The penal slave code usually applied to freedmen. South Carolina, in 1740, im-

---

[224] Thomas R. R. Cobb, op. cit., p. 313.
[225] William Goodell, op. cit., pp. 356–62.

posed a penalty of one hundred dollars on anyone who used a Negro as a scribe or taught him how to write,[226] and this law was further strengthened in 1834 to punish a free person of color by fifty lashes for the same offense.[227] Similar laws were adopted in a number of other states. The law, the church, and social policy all conspired to prevent the identification of the liberated Negro with the community. He was to be kept as a separate, a lesser, being. In spite of being manumitted, he was not considered a free moral agent.

The different slave systems, originating under varying auspices, had achieved sharply contrasting results. If we may use such a term, the milieu in Latin America was expansive and the attitude pliable. The Negro may have been racially a new element, but slavery was a known and recognized institution — known especially to the law. The law had long since struggled with the subtleties of freedom and servitude and over a period of centuries had created an elaborate code for the slave, and the new Negro slave was automatically endowed with the immunities contained in the ancient prescription. He was no stranger to the law. His obligation and freedoms within the code were both known. In fact, *the element of human personality was not lost in the transition to slavery from Africa to the Spanish or Portuguese dominions.*

---

[226] George M. Stroud, op. cit., p. 139.
[227] Ibid., p. 240.

He remained a person even while he was a slave. He lost his freedom, but he retained his right to become free again and, with that privilege, the essential elements in moral worth that make freedom a possibility. He was never considered a mere chattel, never defined as unanimated property, and never under the law treated as such. His master never enjoyed the powers of life and death over his body, even though abuses existed and cruelties were performed. Even if justice proved to be blind, the blindness was not incurable. The Negro slave under this system had both a juridical and a moral personality, even while he was in bondage.

This legal tradition and juridical framework were strengthened by the Catholic religion and were part of its doctrine and practice. It made him a member of the Christian community. It imposed upon both the slave and the master equal obligations to respect and protect the moral personality of the other, and for practical purposes it admitted the slave to the privileges of the sacraments. In the mundane world it meant that marriage was a sacred union that could not be broken by mere caprice, that the slave had a right to his wife, and that the slave's family was, like other families, a recognized union in a moral universe, not different from that of his master's family. Here, again, the religious prescriptions were perhaps as often violated as obeyed. But both the state and the

church combined to maintain the principle of the rule
by the exercise of civil and canon law. The church
could and did thunder its opposition to the sins committed against the family — against all Christian
families, regardless of color and regardless of status.
The church, further, in its emphasis upon the moral
equality between master and slave, came to favor
manumission and to make it a deed laudable in the
sight of God.

The legal right to achieve freedom and the religious favoring of manumission, combined with a number of other features peculiarly American, tended to
make easy the path to freedom. That it was easy is
seen by the large numbers of freedmen everywhere in
Latin America during the colonial period and after
independence.

It was the opinion of de Pons [228] that in the Spanish
colonies there were more freedmen and children of
freedmen than slaves, and he cites for Venezuela,
out of a total population of 728,000, freedmen to the
number of 291,000, or over 40 per cent of the total.
In Cuba, the hundred and three years between 1774
and 1877, for which we seem to have a fairly accurate record, the percentage of freedmen to slaves
never fell below 32 per cent of the slave population,
and in spite of the constant importation of new Ne-

---

[228] F. R. de Pons: *Travels in South America* (2 vols., London,
1807), Vol. I, pp. 168–9.

groes the freedmen were 41 per cent in 1774, and over 55 per cent in 1877.[229] It has been estimated that in Brazil at the time of the emancipation there were three times as many free Negroes as slaves. In contrast, the total of free persons of color in the British West Indies was small. Cuba alone, in 1827, had 20,-000 more free Negroes than all of the British Caribbean islands.[230]

Endowing the slave with a moral personality before emancipation, before he achieved a legal equality, made the transition from slavery to freedom easy, and his incorporation into the free community natural. And as there were always large numbers of freedmen and children of freedmen, it never seemed especially dangerous to increase their number. There was never the question that so agitated people both in the West Indies and in the United States — the danger of emancipation, the lack of fitness for freedom. There was never the horrifying spectacle so often evoked in the United States of admitting a morally inferior and therefore, by implication, a biologically inferior people into the body politic on equal terms.

In this matter of slavery the experience of the nations other than those of the Iberian Peninsula was very different. They had long since lost all vestiges of slavery and a slave code. In neither tradition, pol-

---

[229] Fernando Ortiz, op. cit., pp. 321–2.
[230] William Law Mathieson, op. cit., p. 40.

icy, nor law was there room for the slave. We are told that "In the Eleventh of Elizabeth (1569) one cartwright brought a slave from Russia, and would scourage him, for which he was questioned, and it was resolved, that England was too pure an air for slaves to breathe in." [231] And Cobb generalizes: "That the colonies having adopted the common law, and Negro slavery having no existence in Great Britain, there could be necessarily no provision of that law in reference to it, and consequently the power of the master until limited by legislation was absolute." [232] In neither tradition, policy, nor law was there room for the slave. The law did not know him and could not make provision for him when he came upon the scene. The same is true of public practice and policy. The fact that the slave was a Negro merely added to the confusion; it did not create it. What made the difficulty was that when the first slave was brought in contact with the English, they did not know what to do with him. There was no recognizable place for him in the law. He certainly was not a free man. And the law did not know a slave.

It was therefore no accident that in the early days, both in the West Indies and in the American colonies, he was, in practice, assimilated with the indentured servant. But this effort was of short duration and

[231] John Rushworth: *Historical Collections*, quoted in Helen Tunnicliff Catterall, op. cit., Vol. I, p. 1.
[232] Thomas R. R. Cobb, op. cit., p. 89.

broke down, among other reasons, because the slave
was not an indentured servant. The master had a contractual relation with the indentured servant; there
was no such contractual relation with the Negro slave.
The indentured servant's time was limited by contract to a specified number of years, after which he
was to be free. The master assumed with the indentured servant a certain number of future obligations.
The indentured relationship was recognized by both
sides as temporary and dischargeable by a specified
emolument. The indentured servant was Christian,
had his rights to his wife and children, over whom the
master could exercise no legal compulsions. None of
these terms fitted the slave. He had been bought from
a third person. There was no time limit to the contract, there was no pecuniary obligation upon the master after the contract expired, and, finally, the Negro
slave had no legal family. The master had bought the
slave, the women, and the children, paying separately for each. The slave had no rights in law and acquired none by contract. The legal perplexity was real
enough. This was made worse by the position of the
Protestant churches. The slow, hesitant, and doubt-
ful approach to the problem of conversion merely increased the legal isolation of the Negro within the
community, because as a Christian he would have acquired certain immunities and privileges belonging
to all members of the established church. But the established church was inordinately slow in moving to

bring him into the fold, and the dissident churches were not very successful nor very much respected in their endeavors until nearly the end of slavery as an institution in the West Indies.

In the absence of either religious or legal provision for the slave, it was not illogical for the planters, both in the West Indies and in the American colonies, to settle the legal issue involved by legally defining the slave as chattel. If he was neither a free man nor an indentured servant, then declaring him to be chattel disposed of the puzzle legally. But having once made this decision, the definition of the Negro brought in its train a whole series of consequences, both for the Negro and for the white community, which are reflected even at the present time. For as chattel the Negro slave lost all claims upon legal protection. The powers of the master were enormously increased, and, by definition, the Negro slave was reduced to a beast of the field. While the impact of the law did not and could not completely wipe out the fact that the Negro slave was human, it raised a sufficient barrier to make the humanity of the Negro difficult to recognize and legally almost impossible to provide for. This legal definition carried its own moral consequences and made the ultimate redefinition of the Negro as a moral person most difficult.

The abolition of slavery found both the Negro and the white community unprepared for freedom. In the case of the Negro, there was almost a complete lack of preparation for the responsibilities characteristic of freedom. The number of freedmen was infinitesimal, their role in the free community greatly restricted, and they proved incompetent to absorb and direct the large body of slaves suddenly freed. The denial of a moral status to the slave as a human being was to prove the greatest handicap to drawing the Negro into the general community, and to giving the whites that readiness for the acceptance of the free Negro which would have facilitated the transition. Something of the same course, but much more disastrous in its consequence, worked itself out in the United States. Here, as in the West Indies, the early attempts to identify the slave with the indentured servant broke down and the Negro was reduced to chattel. Here, too, the bias was in favor of slavery and against manumission, and the few Negroes who achieved the status of freedmen were frowned upon, isolated, discriminated against, and even expelled from many of the slave states. All of this does not deny the many thousands of instances of kindness, affection, and understanding between master and slave, but these were personal and with no standing in the law. Legally there was no effective remedy against abuse and no channel toward freedom. With us there were not, as in Brazil, Cuba, and Venezuela, large numbers of freedmen while slavery still existed, and with us the slave had no moral status as a human being, and the Negro no experience in freedom.

The different ways in which slavery was finally abolished in the two areas illumine the social process of which they were an integral part. In the Latin-American area slavery and freedom were, socially and morally speaking, very close to each other. The passage from slavery to freedom was always possible for the individual, and in practice frequent. There was nothing final or inescapable in the slave status. In fact, the contrary was the case. The social structure was malleable, the gap between slavery and freedom narrow and bridgeable, and almost any slave could hope that either he or his family would pass over from his side of the dividing line to the other. Easy manumission all through the period meant that there were always a large number of people in the community who had formerly been slaves and were now free. This is one of the two crucial differences between the character and the outcome of the slave institution in the Latin-American scene on one hand and in the United States on the other. The second basic difference was to be found in the position of the freedman after manumission. In fact, in Latin America there was for legal and practical purposes no separate class of freedmen. The freedman was a free man.[233] In the Latin-American slave system the easy and continuous

---

[233] There were exceptions to this general statement that could be cited in so large an area and for a period of over three centuries, but both law and practice were bent in the direction of giving the Negro, once freed, a free man's rights.

change of status implied a process of evolution and a
capacity for absorption within the social structure that
prevented the society from hardening and kept it from
becoming divided. We are here face to face with an
evolutionary social process that did not allow for a
horizontal stratification and favored passage verti-
cally from slavery to freedom. There is, in fact, from
this point of view, no slave system; there are only
individual slaves. There is no slave by nature, no absolute identification of a given group of individuals
as slaves, to whom and to whose children the hope of
escape from the hardships they are suffering is forever denied.

If in Latin America the abolition of slavery was
achieved in every case without violence, without
bloodshed, and without civil war, it is due to the fact
that there was no such fixed horizontal division, no
such hardening of form that the pattern could no
longer change by internal adaptations. In the Latin-
American area the principle of growth and change
had always been maintained. In the United States the
very opposite had come to pass. For reasons of historical accident and conditioning, the Negro became identified with the slave, and the slave with the eternal
pariah for whom there could be no escape. The slave
could not ordinarily become a free man, and if chance
and good fortune conspired to endow him with freedom, he still remained a Negro, and as a Negro, according to the prevailing belief, he carried all of the

imputation of the slave inside him. In fact, the Negro was considered a slave by nature, and he could not escape his natural shortcomings even if he managed to evade their legal consequences. Freedom was made difficult of achievement and considered undesirable both for the Negro and for the white man's community in which the Negro resided. The distinction had been drawn in absolute terms, not merely between the slave and the free man, but between the Negro and the white man. The contrast was between color — the Negro was the slave, and the white man was the free man. Attributes of a sharply different moral character were soon attached to these different elements in the population, and they became incompatible with each other. They might as well, so far as the theory was concerned, have been of a different species, for all of the things denied to the Negro as a slave were permitted to the white man — as a citizen. Our Southern slave-holding community had by law and custom, by belief and practice, developed a static institutional ideal, which it proceeded to endow with a high ethical bias.

Calhoun stated the case succinctly and forcibly:

It is to us a vital question. It involves not only our liberty, but, what is greater (if to freemen anything can be), existence itself. The relation which now exists between the two races in the slave-holding States has existed for two centuries. It has grown with our growth, and strengthened with our strength. It has entered into and modified all our institutions, civil and political. None other can be substituted. We will not, cannot, permit it to be destroyed. . . . Come what will, should it cost every drop of blood and every cent of property, we must defend ourselves; and if compelled, we would stand justified by all laws, human and divine . . . we would act under an imperious necessity. There would be to us but one alternative, — to triumph or perish as a people. . . . I ask neither sympathy nor compassion for the slave-holding States. We can take care of ourselves. It is not we, but the Union, which is in danger. . . . We cannot remain here in an endless struggle in defence of our character, our property and institutions.[234]

By one of those peculiar tricks which time and experience sometimes play on man, the accident of Negro labor had been converted into a moral and economic philosophy. It seemed to the South that the best of all societies had now been achieved, and by divine prescription it was to remain unchanged forever. But the social milieu had ceased to be pliable and had therefore ceased to be tolerable in the scheme of things. A social pattern no longer open to change has, in fact, quite unconsciously signed its own death warrant. Just at the very moment when the system seems most perfected, when the structure seems most complete, and when inner peace and harmony seem to give the way of life a kind of perfection, the cracks in the structure make their appearance, the fission becomes evident, and the changes so long resisted pre-

[234] Dr. H. von Holst: *John C. Calhoun* (Boston: Houghton, Mifflin & Co.; 1891), p. 133.

cipitate a cataclysm. That only a violent upheaval could change the slavery system in the South was clearly seen by Calhoun:

> To destroy the existing relations would be to destroy this prosperity [of the Southern states], and to place the two races in a state of conflict, which must end in the expulsion or extirpation of one or the other. No other can be substituted compatible with their peace or security. The difficulty is in the diversity of the races. So strongly drawn is the line between the two in consequence, and so strengthened by the force of habit and education, that it is impossible for them to exist together in the community, where their numbers are so nearly equal as in the slave-holding States, under any other relation than that which now exists. Social and political equality between them is impossible. No power on earth can overcome the difficulty. The causes lie too deep in the principles of our nature to be surmounted. But, without such equality, to change the present condition of the African race, were it possible, would be to change the form of slavery.[235]

Revolution is the natural consequence of stratification. The abolition of slavery in the United States was cataclysmic and violent just because it seemed so eternal, so faultless, just because the gap between the Negro and the white man had been made so impassable and so absolute that it could not be bridged by any means of transition, by any natural growth and adaptation. It was broken by violence and war and social catastrophe because it could not be molded by other means. Revolution was the result because

---

[235] Ibid., p. 141.

change as a principle had been denied. The fact that the Civil War was begun on the issue of secession is immaterial. Secession itself was but a final evidence of how stratified the Southern complex had become. It could not change from within, and it was therefore broken by force from without. The great lesson in this experience lies in the eventual outcome inherent in the two slave institutions. The principle of manumission provided Latin-American slavery a means of change. The denial of manumission encrusted the social structure in the Southern states and left no escape except by revolution, which in this case took the form of a civil war.

It is, therefore, not entirely an accident that the abolition of slavery in the United States was achieved within the painful experience of a civil war, and followed by the almost equally painful and disintegrating process of a period of reconstruction.[236]

---

[236] Professor William L. Westermann in a conversation with me has pointed out that when the definition of slavery was symbolized by the Negro, it spelled the death knell of slavery itself within the European cultural area. Slavery is an ancient and universal institution in human experience. It was an accepted, even if not an honored, way of life. The slave was always legally at the bottom of the scale. He had the least claims upon consideration and the fewest prerogatives among living men. But the slave's inferiority was largely legal rather than moral. Certainly that was true in the Greek city-state period and in the ancient world after the days of the Middle Stoic group and the early Christian fathers. Anyone might become a slave — the accidents of war or poverty might force even the best men into the position of belonging to

The Civil War gave the Negro legal equality with his former masters, but it could not and did not give him either the experience in the exercise of freedom or the moral status in the sight of his white fellow citizens to make the freedom of the Negro an accept-

another, either temporarily or permanently. It was a misfortune when it occurred. It was not an evidence of baseness, except in cases where men were made slaves as a punishment for crime. But, in any case, slavery was of a nature that was independent of race, or even of class, for a soldier belonging to the "best family" might be taken in war and enslaved.

Slavery had no identification until modern time with any one race. As a general rule in antiquity it did not involve the assumption of congenital or racial inferiority. But when, as a result of the discovery of the Western World, the people out of Africa were forced to migrate to the other side of the Atlantic by many millions, slavery and the Negro came to be synonymous. The Negro became the slave. The Indian, except under very restricted circumstances, and only for a very few years, was also a slave, but for all practical purposes the slave and the black man were identifiable in the minds of the Europeans and people of European culture.

The results of this change were unexpected. For one thing, slavery became a moral issue, something it had never been before. If only the Negro could be a slave — only the Negro and no one else — the question soon arose: why the Negro? A whole series of explanations was soon devised to justify slavery for the Negro. The justifications were numerous and many-sided, finding support in Biblical as well as presumably scientific sources. But the mere fact that slavery had to be justified left the question open to doubt. Men began to ask, why the Negro? On what grounds and for what reasons? If slavery is just, then it must include other peoples as well; otherwise it was not acceptable to the conscience of Europe, at least to the extent of fully quieting Europe's conscience on the matter. And if reasons could be adduced on one

able and workable relationship for them. The endowing of the Negro with a legal equality left a moral
vacuum that remained to be filled in. In Latin America the Negro achieved complete legal equality
slowly, through manumission, over centuries, and
after he had acquired a moral personality. In the
United States he was given his freedom suddenly,
and before the white community credited him with
moral status.

Herein lies the great contrast between the outcome
of the two slave systems. The last eighty years in the
United States may be characterized as a period within
which the Negro has been struggling for moral status
in the sight of the white community. It has been a
painful and, for the Negro, often a disillusioning effort. But it cannot be denied that progress has been

side, they could also be adduced on the other. The entire question of slavery itself as a moral institution came to be questioned
and finally repudiated. As long as slavery was something that anyone might suffer, then it could be looked upon as a misfortune.
When it became identified solely with the Negro, then it became
a matter of doubt whether any man ought to be permitted to
suffer it. Interestingly enough, the Negro himself became a party
to the argument and denied the imputation that he, of all people,
had been selected to be the eternal pariah of the race. Educated
Negroes in some countries became important in the agitation
against slavery. Slavery was therefore finally abolished for the
Negro, within the European frame of reference, on moral
grounds, because it was unjust that any one race should be so
singled out. When Negro slavery was abolished, slavery was abolished. The issue had been so stated during the agitation over Negro
slavery that by implication all slavery had become unjust.

made, and the moral position of the Negro within the American community is today much better than it was in 1865, the day after the Emancipation.

One must always remember that the Negro started after the Civil War with nothing at all; he had neither education, nor property, nor position, nor the psychological readiness for achievement and personal growth. To have gone so far and to have accomplished so much in eighty years is a very great accomplishment indeed. To have done it against the prejudice, denial, and opposition with which his path has been strewn bespeaks both spiritual resilience and purposefulness. The record in the face of the same kind of handicaps has probably never been equaled before.

It is true, however, that the achievement is also evidence of a pliability in the American milieu, and an indication that belief in the right of all men to equal opportunity is not mere lip service. At least, one would have to say that the American environment since the Civil War was provided a permissive setting, so that some of the least privileged, as the Negro has been, could prove their worth and find access to the best that the culture has had to offer. But the test of acceptance lies in a somewhat different direction. The issue is a subtle one and hard to state. It is not enough to say, as we often do, that there are so many Negro doctors, lawyers, politicians, business men, and scholars. It is requisite that there should not be Negro doctors, Negro lawyers, or Negro scholars. Their professional standing must overshadow their racial origin. It is only when we can say he is a great actor, a great scholar, a great lawyer, a great citizen that the step has been taken which endows the Negro with the moral worth as a man which obliterates the invidious distinction and sweeps away the condescending fawning of the better-than-thou attitude. When the time does come that a Negro judge on the bench is a judge and not a Negro judge, when a Negro scholar is a scholar and not a Negro scholar, then the process of identification will be on its way to fulfillment, and the gap between legal equality and moral acceptance will be obliterated.

The pointing up of racial conflicts and injustices is important. But the frictions are a healthy sign. They indicate a many-sided contact between the two races. The frictions are an evidence of the fact that the Negro and the white man live in the same community and quarrel over the same values. As long as the two races are striving and disagreeing over the manifold issues of living in the same culture, then it means that they are engaged in the painful process of accommodation to each other and to the world. The real danger would be if the Negro managed to live in a vacuum where there was no friction between him and his white neighbors; then there would be real danger of the developing of a perpetual caste system. It is desirable that nothing should remain static until the issues over which the friction arises have themselves ceased to trouble either the whites or the blacks. To want peace when the contrasts are so great is to dream of an unreal world. To expect either the white or the Negro community to show neither anger nor hate, neither fear nor violence, when their values are challenged and their aspirations are frustrated is to ask for the impossible. It is not specific evils that we must complain of — they are to be dealt with by the police and public authorities. It is the general direction which gives the evils their pertinence that is the significant issue, and, from that point of view, the friction is a good thing. It shows that the evils complained of are alive, troublesome, and impelling. They force men to do something about them. They will do many wrong things about them, but, by the same token, many right ones.

The nature of our problem is conditioned by the time it will take for the Negro to have acquired a moral personality equal to his legal one. How long that will take is not predictable, but what is generally called the "solution" of the Negro problem is essentially a matter of establishing the Negro in the sight of the white community as a human being equal to its own members. When that finally occurs, then the problem will have solved itself. It will have disappeared. But such an eventuality is a matter of time, and here, too, the Spanish and Portuguese peoples have a great advantage over the Americans. They have lived with the Negro much longer than we have. Negroes were first brought to Portugal in 1442, and in considerable numbers following that date, while the first Negro slaves to reach Virginia came in 1619, a hundred and seventy-seven years later. It will be the year 2122 before the Americans will have had as long a contact with the Negro as the Latin Americans now have. Taking the progress that has been made in the eighty years since the Emancipation, there is some hope that the Negro will, in time, have achieved in the United States as good a relationship as he now enjoys in Latin America. In fact, it may not be unreasonable to assume that the Negro in the United States, because of the greater opportunities available in our midst, will have forged a position no less favorable morally, and economically better, long before he has filled the time span during which he has sojourned among the Iberian people.

This will be easier because, in spite of the sharp contrast here drawn, the slave systems in Latin and Anglo-Saxon America were not institutions differing absolutely one from the other. Differences there were, and important ones, but they were differences of degree rather than in kind. The institution of slavery had logic of its own. Wherever it existed in this hemisphere it worked its way into the social structure and modified the total society. The slave system was broader in its impact than might be discerned from a reading of the slave laws. The law itself was but evidence of the influence of slavery as an institution upon the *mores*. In fact, so inclusive was the influence of slavery that it might be better to speak, not of a system of slavery in Brazil, Cuba, or the United States, but of the total pattern as a slave society. Slavery was not something apart from the world in which it existed. It was merely one facet of the world and cannot, in its influence, be separated from or described apart from the total community. Wherever we had slavery, we had a slave society, not merely for the blacks, but for the whites, not merely for the law, but for the family, not merely for the labor system, but for the culture — the total culture. Nothing escaped, nothing was beyond or above or outside the slave institution; the institution was the society in all of its manifestations.

The social structure is dynamic and not static. In spite of every effort so to define the role of the Negro as to make him chattel or real estate for the purpose of legal treatment, he was still a human being. The Negro, by his presence, changed the form of the state, the nature of property, the system of law, the organization of labor, the role of the church as well as its character, the notions of justice, ethics, ideas of right and wrong. Slavery influenced the architecture, the clothing, the cooking, the politics, the literature, the morals of the entire group — white and black, men and women, old and young. Nothing escaped, nothing, and no one. Everywhere in this New World of ours a slave system made a slave society, with all of the *mores* of a slave society. Important as the differences between Brazil and the United States were, the similarities were undoubtedly greater. Slavery proved a pervasive influence that enveloped all of life and patterned it in a way peculiar to itself.

It is a problem both in theory and in fact. In theory we must say that any change occurring in any part of the social structure affects the entire society. That is true even if the particular society has a rigid class or caste system. Any influence that affects the lowest stratum makes its way upwards and modifies the highest caste. There is no such thing as isolating or segregating a social phenomenon. It works its way throughout the whole society. All social influences are vertical. No matter where they occur or of what particular nature they may be — crime, prostitution, slavery, literacy, trade unions, beliefs, public schools, or denominational variants in the religious organization, or system of political theory and scientific concepts — they all tend to influence the total structure; and they do so by vertical penetration, so that any awareness, approval, denial, or rejection is evidence of the influence. And in the realm of fact — of mere physical fact — the presence of the human beings who are the carriers of the particular influence is also vertical. The slave who attends his lady on her way to church, the master's son who finds a young colored mistress, with or without the knowledge of his parents, the Negro slave who sings his doleful songs and influences the music, the rhythm, the range of musical awareness of his masters, even against their will or, better still, without their conscious knowledge of what is occurring, affect the total culture.

There was always, in any slave society in this hemisphere, a vertical flow from below, not merely of ethical, religious, and purely cultural traits, but biologically as well. The slave always — the Negro slave always — broke through the upper crust in some measure and penetrated in greater or lesser degree, with or without the consent of the law, in spite of the law, in spite of the social *mores,* in spite of every restraint, objection, condemnation, and punishment. Biological as well as social mobility existed, and the flow upward overcame distinctions not merely in caste but in race. The law and the milieu differed sharply in Latin America and the British West Indies and the United States, but the end result has proved to be the same in greater or lesser degree, and the direction is unmistakable. The dynamics of human life and culture have proved more persistent and more continuous than the theory or the law. Gilberto Freyre speaks of the social and even the racial mobility of Brazil as something that has proved acceptable, even as something of a matter of pride.[237] Portuguese colonization produced a fluid structure, making possible the trans-

---

[237] Gilberto Freyre: *O Mundo que o Portugues Criou* (Rio de Janeiro, 1940), p. 57.

mutation from class to class, from race to race, and producing a new biological type, and new values in human beauty. The mixture of races in Brazil was certainly persistent, and accepted, and broad in its reach. The wealthy upper-class slave-owner with his seraglio of slave women on one side, and the poorer, isolated *fazendero* in the backwoods on the other, both participated in the universal process of miscegenation:

When I had finished, he invited me to his porch, where he brought me some excellent coffee, and set a mulatto of his establishment on an opposite bench, to play on the guitar for my amusement. He then called forth and introduced me to his whole family. This consisted of two mothers, a black and a white, and twelve children, of all sizes, sexes and colors; some with woolly hair and dusky faces, some with sallow skins and long black tresses. In a short time, they made up a ball, and began to dance. It was opened by the youngest, Luzia, a child of about four years old, with dark eyes, and coal black hair. She was presently joined by a little black sister, and they commenced with a movement, resembling a Spanish bolero, imitating admirably well the castanets with their fingers and thumbs. The movement of the dance was not very delicate; and the children, when they began, showed a certain timidity and innate consciousness that they were exhibiting before a stranger what was not proper; but by degrees they were joined in succession by all the children, boys and girls, up to the age of seventeen and eighteen, and finally by the two mothers of the progeny. I never saw such a scene. I was realizing what I had heard of the state of families in the midst of woods, shut out from intercourse with all other society, and forming promiscuous connexions with one another, as if they were in an early age of the world, and had

no other human beings to attach themselves to. I had person-
ally known some, and I had heard of others, brothers and
sisters, who without scruple or sense of shame, lived together,
supporting in other respects the decencies of life; but here it
was carried beyond what I could have supposed possible, and
this precocious family displayed among themselves dances,
resembling what we have heard of the Otaheitan Timordee.
I soon retired, but the sound of the guitar continued a long
time after.[238]

The process of miscegenation was part of the system of slavery, and not just of Brazilian slavery. The
biological transmutation from one race toward another, the new type of beauty, the new race was being
evolved everywhere. The dynamics of race contact
and sex interest were stronger than prejudice, theory,
law, or belief. The difference was that in Brazil it was
accepted as a matter of course and has come to be, to
a certain extent, a point of pride.

A sense of racial vigor and cultural dynamism is
ascribed to the influence of this mixture of races. In
other places, in the British and French West Indies
and in the United States, it was frowned upon, for-
bidden by law, denied, and condemned, but it went on
just the same. Perhaps not to the same degree, but
who knows? And the long-run consequences are not
so greatly different as is presumed. In the British
West Indies miscegenation was widely practiced,
much to the chagrin of the righteous people. But it
went on, and even the "better" people — or their

---

[238] Rev. R. Walsh, op. cit., Vol. II, p. 137.

sons — became a party to the process. The dynamics
of social life and human contact have an intimacy that
is beyond circumscription by the law. Even so staid
and formal a historian as Bryan Edwards finds himself confessing the fact: "The accusation generally
brought against the free people of colour, is the in-
continency of their women; of whom, such as are
young and have tolerable persons, are universally
maintained by white men of all ranks and conditions,
as kept mistresses. The fact is too notorious to be con-
cealed or controverted. . . ."[239] The young men
brought over from Great Britain as overseers of the
plantations did not marry — they took colored mistresses:

It is a well-known and notorious fact, that very few of the
white men in the West Indies marry, except a few professional men and some few merchants in the towns, and here
and there, in the country, a proprietor or large attorney.
Most of the merchants and shopkeepers in the towns, and the
whole of the deputy planters, (viz., overseers) in all parts of
the country, have what is called a housekeeper, who is their
concubine or mistress, and is generally a free woman of
colour; but the book-keepers, who are too poor and too dependent to have any kind of establishment, generally take
some mulatto, or black female slave, from the estate where
they are employed, or live in a more general state of licentiousness.[240]

---

[239] Bryan Edwards, op. cit., Vol. II, p. 221.
[240] R. Bickell, op. cit., p. 104.

So notorious was the practice and so constant the fact that a special term arose to describe the white man who had become submerged on the plantation among his Negro servants and concubines. He had become, as the expression was, "a white Negro." [241]

This same mingling of the races and classes occurred in the United States. The record is replete with the occurrence, in spite of law, doctrine, and belief. Every traveler in the South before the Civil War comments on the widespread miscegenation, and a whole volume could be filled with extracts like the following:

If Joe Smith had been born and brought up in the Slave States, he would never have thought of being the founder of a sect. Among the million of female chattels in the South, the supply would have been equal to the demand. You never hear of free-love associations in the South. From the very structure of slave society there is no necessity for them. . . . Amalgamation is increasing at a horrible rate throughout the slave states; and will continue to increase while wealth and luxury prevail in one class of the community and degradation in the other. There are many pure and virtuous men in the South, who are, and who have been so, even from their childhood; but . . . they labor under a temptation twofold greater than persons who occupy the same social position in the free states. It is admitted, by truthful men in the South, that slavery is a source of unbounded licentiousness. . . . It is with pain that I express the conviction that one of the rea-

[241] Mrs. A. C. Carmichael: *Domestic Manners of the West Indies* (London: Whittaker, Treacher, & Co.; 1833), Vol. I, p. 59.

sons why wicked men in the South uphold slavery is the facility which it affords for a licentious life. Negroes tell no tales in courts of law of the violation by white men of colored females.[242]

Miscegenation went on among all classes in the community, and the racial and class mobility was as characteristic in Southern slave states as in other slave societies in this hemisphere. The mulatto in the United States, like the mulatto in other places, is the child of a white father and a dark mother, and it has been said somewhere that in the United States there are not more than ten per cent of the colored population who have no admixture of white blood flowing through their veins.

One of the many consequences of miscegenation proved to be the inevitable differentiation between the mulatto and the pure black, a differentiation that differed in degree rather than in kind in the different slave systems. It not only produced social distinction in the colored part of the population, but brought a part of the population closer to the master. Even in the British West Indies it was customary not to put mulattoes to work in the sugarcane fields, but rather to keep them as house servants and put them to learn skilled trades; and it was expected that a white man

---

[242] Rev. J. D. Long, of Maryland, 1857, quoted by Arthur W. Calhoun in *A Social History of the American Family, from Colonial Times to the Present* (Cleveland: Arthur H. Clark Co.; 1918), Vol. II, pp. 295–6.

would free his mulatto child, and when he did not do so, the father was "most justly detested, and held up as a character anything but respectable." [243] In the United States the opposition to manumission was so great in many states that it was difficult for a white father to free his children even if he wanted to. But the fact is that such children were occasionally freed, and there are hundreds of cases in the court records of legal battles over the inheritance of property by the mulatto children of white fathers. The law did not favor manumission, and the courts were perhaps inclined to favor the white claimant against the mulatto heir. But the fact remains that even in our system it proved impossible to suppress completely the natural tendency toward racial and class mobility. Looking back, it seems perfectly clear that the mobility begun on a physical basis has gradually and inevitably spread to the political, cultural, and social fields. In the West Indies, where the whites were so proud and so arrogant and so sure of themselves, the racial and social fluidity has proved almost complete.

The leaders of the community are often coloured men, the children of the mixed marriages which many are wont to deplore. . . .

The strata of coloured West Indian Society are already complex. A few at the top, judges, barristers, doctors, whatever their shades of colour, could hold their own in any circle.

---

[243] Mrs. A. C. Carmichael, op. cit., Vol. I, p. 91.

A great many more are the intellectual equals or superiors of their own white contemporaries.[244]

And the same has occurred in the French West Indies:

On the other hand, the "little whites," clerks, secretaries, government officials, agents, are now thrust aside, unable to compete with their Negro and mulatto rivals. Officials swarm just as much in the English as in the other islands, and in virtue of their very numbers the men of colour get elected to most of the subordinate posts. In certain districts the whites, refusing the administration of the sons of slaves, have completely disappeared. In this struggle for existence probably more than one-fourth of the European element has been eliminated since the middle of the century.

Their successful rivals are no longer full-blood Negroes, but mulattoes or "people of colour." Miscegenation has become universal despite the unfavourable initial conditions and the severe laws formerly interdicting such alliances. At present the insular populations present every conceivable transition from sallow white to glossy black, though the prevalent hue is a brown yellow, a fine bronze tint, or even that of pale gold. Certainly this mixed race has not declined, and the half-caste creoles especially of Martinique and Dominica are amongst the finest in the Antilles.[245]

The achievement of the Negroes in the United States has already been noticed. The import of all this discussion is merely to point out the fact that the

---

[244] W. M. Macmillan: *Warning from the West Indies*, op. cit., p. 48.

[245] Elisée Reclus: *The Universal Geography*, edited by A. H. Keane (London: J. S. Virtue and Co.), Vol. III, p. 462.

institution of slavery was inevitably mobile, that it had a logic of its own broader than any system of law, or custom, tradition, or belief. What the law and tradition did was to make the social mobility easy and natural in one place, difficult and slow and painful in another. In Brazil and Spanish America the law, the church, and custom put few impediments in the way of vertical mobility of race and class, and in some measure favored it. In the British, French, and United States slave systems the law attempted to fix the pattern and stratify the social classes and the racial groups. But the law failed. The Haitian rebellion, the Civil War in the United States, and the abolition of slavery in the British West Indies are all part of the same process.

A stratified society, at least in terms of the experience of this hemisphere, that will not leave open a channel for growth, change, and modulation will be changed by force. So it happened. But more important than that is the fact so clearly revealed that the underlying social process was similar under slavery in this hemisphere regardless of the ægis under which it originated. Physical proximity, slow cultural intertwining, the growth of a middle group that stands in experience and equipment between the lower and the upper class, and the slow process of moral identification work their way against all seemingly absolute systems of values and prejudices. Society is essentially dynamic, and while the mills of God grind slow, they grind exceeding sure. Time — the long time — will draw a veil over the white and black in this hemisphere, and future generations will look back upon the record of strife as it stands revealed in the history of the people of this New World of ours with wonder and incredulity. For they will not understand the issues that the quarrel was about.

INDEX

viii